Innovative Business Projects

Breaking Complexities, Building Performance

Volume One
Fundamentals and Project Environment

Rajagopal

Professor,
EGADE Business School
Tecnologico de Monterrey
Mexico City, Mexico
&
Visiting Professor,
Department of Administrative Sciences,
Boston University, Boston, MA

BEP BUSINESS EXPERT PRESS

*Innovative Business Projects: Breaking Complexities, Building Performance,
Volume One: Fundamentals and Project Environment*

First published in 2017 by
Business Expert Press, LLC
222 East 46th Street, New York, NY 10017
www.businessexpertpress.com

ISBN-13: 978-1-63157-529-7 (paperback)
ISBN-13: 978-1-63157-530-3 (e-book)

Business Expert Press Portfolio and Project Management Collection

Collection ISSN: 2156-8189 (print)
Collection ISSN: 2156-8200 (electronic)

Cover and interior design by Exeter Premedia Services Private Ltd.,
Chennai, India

First edition: 2017

10 9 8 7 6 5 4 3 2 1

Printed in the United States of America.

With love to Arati,
who inspires me to take up new projects and encourages
to deliver the best performance

Abstract

This book examines and emphasizes the project design and operations process across the business cultures, the requirements to carry business projects successfully and implement the project plans carefully. One of the core arguments this book presents is that the right decisions support planning and implementation of business projects, accelerates its process, and lower the risk with the measurable results in the rapidly growing international marketplace. In the growing market competition in the 21st century, corporate success depends on breaking through the innovation-oriented business projects and analyzing the right information for building marketplace strategies. However, it is evident from the failures of several corporate initiatives that most companies are unable to manage business projects efficiently. This book presents new insights on developing competitive business project designs and breakthroughs in managing them, considering the time, territory, target, and tasks management, assuring business gains and market competitiveness.

Keywords

business projects, commercialization, consumer behavior, global marketplace, innovation management, market competitiveness, project management, technology management

Contents

Preface xi

Acknowledgments.. xv

Chapter 1   Thinking Out of the Box..1

Chapter 2   Analyzing Business Scenario..37

Chapter 3   Setting Up Innovative Business Projects 73

Chapter 4   Project Environment..113

Chapter 5   Administering Business Projects 147

Index 189

Preface

The growing competitive dynamics in the markets engage firms working with diversified business projects to drive high performance and gain competitive advantage in the market. Managing multiple business projects breeds uncertainty in project operations, causes failures, and damages the corporate credibility. The conventional project management no longer guarantees the success of complex business projects, such as technology-driven new products. As companies contemplate sustained growth in the global marketplace, it is essential to manage their business projects efficiently by minimizing the risk and maximizing the project output. In an effort to design, develop, and manage client-led business projects, companies working as original equipment manufacturers should learn managing projects with lean techniques to avoid the cost and time overrun, lowering the performance of the project output toward productivity, competence, market competitiveness, and profitability.

The business projects require balanced management of both the technical and behavioral issues. This book addresses the project management tools and techniques in reference to innovation management, public equity management, new product development and its launch management, and managing production and marketing projects in the broad range of industries where project management principles can be applied. It focuses on how project management can be integrated to the organizational performance as a whole. In the marketplace today, speed of strategy implementation is important to gain the first-mover advantage, but at the same time, only the companies that are able to make right strategic choice are found fit to do business in the international destinations. In order to achieve these attributes, companies need to develop right business projects, engage in the stage-gate process meticulously, and deliver the project outcome. Successful companies invest enormous resources on developing sustainable business projects, considering competitive gains within the company, market, or industry.

This book examines and emphasizes the project design and operations process across the business cultures, the requirements to carry business projects successfully, and implement the project plans carefully. One of the core arguments this book presents is that the right decisions support planning and implementation of business projects, accelerate business innovations process, and lower the risk with the measurable results in the rapidly growing international marketplace. In the growing market competition in the 21st century, corporate success depends on breaking through the innovation-oriented business projects and analyzing the right information for building marketplace strategies. However, it is evident from the failures of several corporate initiatives that most companies are unable to manage business projects efficiently. This book presents new insights on developing competitive business project designs and break-throughs in managing them, considering time, territory, target, and tasks management, assuring business gains and market competitiveness.

Well-managed companies meticulously develop innovative business projects by carrying out comprehensive analysis of market information, resources, organizational competencies and capabilities, and market attributes. The innovative business projects help companies in developing manufacturing and operations dexterity, managing economies of scale, distribution, pricing, and promotion management. Any new enterprise in the global marketplace needs strong management skills for business projects to develop innovation, competitiveness, and application of technology for sustainable growth. A fundamental challenge in managing innovative business projects, particularly in large diversified global companies, is choosing the right research design, using right data analysis techniques, managing resources, and drawing desired outcomes.

This volume of the book is divided into five chapters, illustrated with the figures and examples that help readers to easily get the concept and approach of innovative business projects. Chapter 1 discusses the contemporary trend of managing innovation projects and converging local-global enterprises by thinking out-of-the-box to gain win-win advantages through the project deliverables in the market. This chapter discusses competitive differentiation, global innovation trends, lessons learned by the large companies involving start-up enterprises in managing innovative business projects, critical success factors in managing innovation projects, and the outgrowth of patterns of innovations in emerging markets at the low-end markets. Chapter 2 analyzes the business scenario and discusses the ways to explore innovative business projects that have the potential to commercialize and sustain the market competition. This chapter addresses various perspectives of managing innovation projects right from the ways of defining and managing projects to understanding consumers for innovation adaptation, and examines the macro- and microeconomic factors as a part of business scenario of the innovation projects. The systematic discussion on establishing new innovative business projects is presented in Chapter 3, which addresses the concepts of innovation entrepreneurship and illustrates entrepreneurial attributes. This chapter also ponders over the perspectives of resource and cost management and work breakdown structure in managing the innovation projects. The market development for innovative projects, lean thinking in innovation projects, and constituting project teams have also been addressed in this chapter. The project environment is different from the business scenario in managing a project. This important topic has been argued with contemporary knowledge explaining the external and internal fit, transfer of innovation and technology, project matrix, project lifecycle, and managing competitiveness in the innovation projects, in a broad leaning setup of Chapter 4. The most imperative topic on administering business projects is discussed in Chapter 5, which critically examines the development of project scope, documenting project charter, analyzing innovation lifecycle, and determining the use of critical path analysis required for effective administration of business projects. Besides other factors of project administration, this chapter also addresses the application of the stage-gate process in the project administration and discusses categorically cognitive factors in entrepreneurial performance.

The thought process in evolving this book originated from the course on Innovation, Technology and National Economic Development, which I have been teaching at Boston University since 2013. Consequent to teaching this course, I have authored the book "Architecting Enterprise: Managing Innovation, Technology, and Global Competitiveness," and over a short span, another book "The Butterfly Effect in Competitive Markets: Driving Small Changes for Larger Differences" was authored by me in 2015. This book "Innovative Business Projects: Breaking

Complexities, Building Performance" in two volumes is an outgrowth of all the preceding reading, writings, deliveries, and learning. This book reviews categorically the project management theories, concepts, and previous researches, and discusses the applied tools and techniques for business projects. The book discusses contemporary project management approaches for the companies to grow competitive along with the market players and consumers. This book significantly contributes to the existing literature and serves as a learning post and a think tank for students, researchers, and business managers.

Rajagopal
June 01, 2016
Mexico City

Acknowledgments

In completing this volume of the book, I have benefitted from the discussions of my colleagues within and outside the EGADE Business School. I am thankful to Dr. Kip Becker and Dr. John Sullivan of Administrative Sciences Department of Boston University, and Dr. Maria de Lourdes Dieck Assad, Dean of EGADE Business School, who have always encouraged me to take up new challenges in teaching graduate courses, develop new insights, and contribute to the existing literature prolifically. I thank all my students at Boston University for sharing enriching ideas during the classroom discussions that helped in building this book on the framework of innovative ideas.

I also acknowledge the outstanding support of Stewart Mattson, Executive VP and Chief Operating Officer, and Scott Isenberg, Executive Acquisitions Editor, of Business Expert Press, who critically examined the proposal, guided the manuscript preparation, and took the publication process forward. My special thanks to Timothy J. Kloppenborg, Professor Emeritus from Williams College of Business, Xavier University for his guidance and encouragement in bringing out the two volumes of this book. I am thankful to various anonymous referees of my previous research works on innovation and technology management, who helped in looking deeper into the conceptual gaps and improving the quality of the content with their valuable feedback.

Finally, I express my deep gratitude to my beloved wife Arati Rajagopal who has been instrumental in completing this book like all other works of mine. I acknowledge her help in copyediting the first draft of the manuscript and for staying in touch until the final proofs were crosschecked and the index was developed.

CHAPTER 1

Thinking Out of the Box

Overview

Globalization has driven competition and new challenges among firms to sustain in the marketplace. The innovation business projects in most companies follow a boom-bust cycle. As the economy prospers, companies invest substantial resources in developing innovation projects to lead in the competitive markets, while they rethink their priorities in view of the cost-benefit ratios when the markets soars. Growing firms are engaged in developing competitive strategies and innovative differentiations in staying sustainable and competitive in the global marketplace. In order to gain competitive advantages, companies explore innovative business projects to enter the new market segments with first-mover advantages. This chapter discusses the key indicators of globalization and business environment that need to be analyzed by the companies in order to develop innovative business projects to drive competitive differentiation among various consumer segments. Creating competitive advantages for innovating companies does make a difference by pulling the entire eco-system into a creative conversation and developing a challenging business project with innovative differentiation. Leaders, who put all the pieces together, will have a huge advantage as innovation trends, lessons from business projects, and critical success factors of innovative business in the emerging markets have been critically examined in this chapter.

Globalization and Business Environment

Globalization has become a functional dynamics of the emerging firms in the business environment today. Most firms believe that globalization is a synonym to business growth, and invest perennial resources in developing strategy for going global. It has become one of the most pertinent issues for managers of growing firms around the world. In the process of evolving global, many forces drive local enterprises to globalize by expanding their brand reach and participating in foreign markets through various modes of entry. In developed countries, domestic markets have turned mature and are demanding to seek international markets, while in some countries like Brazil, Russia, India, and China, most companies in the present competitive marketplace are found to be born global. A large number of companies in the United States has been nourished by the huge domestic market, but they typically lag behind their European and Japanese rivals in internationalization. *Born global* firms hold dynamic growth in the competitive marketplace and achieve substantial international sales from an early stage in their development, despite economic and technological constraints. They internationalize rapidly as the period from domestic establishment to initial foreign market entry is often three years or less. Born global firms are emerging in sizable numbers worldwide. Until recently, international business was mainly the domain of large, well-resourced multinational enterprises. The appearance of large numbers of born global firms is revolutionizing the traditional character of international business and helping to reshape the global economy (Cavusgil and Knight 2009). Companies intending to go global exhibit two apparent objectives—one is to take advantage of opportunities for growth and expansion, while the other is survival in the business amidst growing competition. However, firms that fail to pursue global opportunities will eventually lose their domestic markets and may be pushed aside by stronger and more competitive global firms. In the process of going global, firms need to adopt innovative marketing strategy to sustain against competing firms. Most firms follow a global perspective to expand their business across the destinations instead of adopting a country-by-country or region-by-region perspective in developing a marketing strategy (Rajagopal 2014).

The need for competitive differentiation through continuous innovation to attract new customers and retain the existing ones has become a major challenge for the companies to sustain in the markets across geo-demographic destinations in the world today. Businesses constantly innovate to augment the stakeholder value, and deliver competitive advantages to the customer through innovation and technology breakthroughs. The customer-centric companies are engaged in developing innovative business projects not only to increase customer value in the competitive marketplace, but also to gain sustainable market share of their products and services. Innovation-driven companies are thinking afresh about capturing more value and also encouraging the start-up ventures by proving seed capital to bring innovation to business using technology and human resources. In the splurge of globalization, dynamic companies tend to spot the innovation opportunities that provide them the first-mover advantage at low cost, and leverage customer value. The innovation, thus, commonly begins with small start-up enterprises (SUEs) and is later nurtured by large companies that establish the competitive difference in the marketplace (Michel 2014).

Along with the growth of information technology, small entrepreneurial ventures are developing rapidly in the 21st century for providing business support to the large companies within the industry. A start-up company is a low-resource and small-size enterprise, or a partnership organization designed to search for an innovative and scalable business model. These companies are generally newly created, innovative in the process of development, and are engaged in customer-centric research for target markets. The start-up companies are largely located in the emerging markets and have become internationally widespread during the dot-com bubble when a great number of Internet-based companies were founded. The start-up companies are often assumed to be solely technology-based companies aiming to go global with enormous ambition, innovation, scalability, and growth.

Going global is an easy process for firms. Firms need to simulate the impact of their business in global market in reference to their resources, target markets, and operational efficiency. Most firms concentrate on product markets considering that the customers seek benefits or want to be served with the same products, services, innovation, and technology, regardless of the geo-demographic differences and cognitive behavior. There are a number of paradoxes in communicating the product-marketing strategies in global marketplace. For example, in advertising products and services in the global marketplace, paradoxical values may emerge within and between cultures. It is necessary for the firms evolving to global scale to understand that markets are people, not products. There may be global products, but there are not global people; hence, firms need to adopt the consumer-centric marketing approach in the global marketplace, rather than going rampant in employing strategies to outmaneuver or outperform the competitors in the market-place (Svensson 2002; Rajagopal 2012).

Globalization has driven the economic philosophy of governments of many developing countries toward industrialization by allowing large multinational corporations and major financial institutions to help local companies and shape the national economy together. Various digital platforms serving to improve the business performance have widened the global reach of local business by encompassing entrepreneurs, business application developers, and small businesses, which are growing as ancillary to the large companies. Globalization, on a positive measure, has established a common thread in economic growth and instituted new-industrial revolution since the mid-20th century. The industrial revolution is driven by continuous innovation to drive competitive differentiation in business today through the movement of goods, services, finance, and people. Global flows are bonding new levels of connectedness among economies and playing an ever-larger role in determining the economic growth and companies.

Globalization and its impacts have profound implications for a broad range of issues important to the funding community. These issues range from the sustainable use of the worlds' resources and the protection and preservation of the environment, to the need to improve living standards, safeguard human rights, promote and protect cultures, and ensure democratic and responsive global governance. Globalization of market opportunities was observed as the outgrowth of the aforementioned factors, and the scope of such marketing opportunities has increased with the continued deregulation of the significant functional sectors like financial services, leisure industry, information technology, and so on.

Most companies have adopted international expansion as a strategy by implementing the innovation projects across the geo-demographic market segments to take advantage of business opportunities. The companies prospecting to succeed in the competitive marketplace commonly set objectives as increasing revenue, bypassing hypercompetitive or saturated home market by striking innovative differentiation, and entering in an emerging or lucrative market. In the global markets, companies leverage their leadership capabilities by continuous innovation and improving their business performance against dynamic competition. However, success of business expansion in international markets is not guaranteed with conventional wisdom. The variety of factors that lead to business failures include lack of understanding of the purchasing characteristics of consumers, underestimation of the local competition, lack of innovation, supply chain issues, and poor strategic decisions, and the business analytics of expansion. However, Aldo, Carrefour, and Nordstrom were successful in the global marketplace as they understood customer preferences and focused on location advantages and customer-centric innovations (Yoder, Visich, and Rustambekov 2016).

Globalization has increased the access to the markets as the remote markets have been reduced following the political and economic changes worldwide. The market access has also been improved by the growing trade blocks at the regional level. Such accessibility to the markets is further reinforced by reducing the trade barriers through far-reaching business communication strategies, product and market development programs, and customer relations. This situation has given a boost in determining the market opportunities as narrowing the trade barriers helped in deregulating certain sectors of trade, such as financial services. The technical operating standards and protocols are being widely adapted to synchronize with the global industry standards. The resources are managed externally to a large extent as the best and low-cost materials are procured locally by the multinational companies. The benefits of global sourcing for such companies include low-cost labor, uniform quality, innovative ideas, access to local markets, economies of scale, lower taxes and duties, lower logistics costs, and more consistent supply. However, there are also some risks in global sourcing that might be political, economic, exchange, or supplier risks. In globalization, the product lifecycles are getting shorter as the new products are penetrating with higher speed in the markets due to technological development and scale of operations. In this process, many products are dropped off the product lifecycle either at the stage of introduction or growth. There are few products that sustain till the mature stage is passed. The growth of technology and its dynamic synchronization with the industry is converging fast, leading toward quick adaptations of global products. The globalization of customer requirements is resulting from the identification of world-wide customer segments of homogeneous preferences across the territorial boundaries.

Business-to-consumers and business-to-business markets are powered by the consumer demands from the global companies, as they are perceived more value-oriented and of added benefits. Innovation and technology played a pivotal role in opening the global avenues for the regional firms.

As globalization marches onward, the multinational companies have shown the trend of continuous expansion to the newer geo-demographic destinations by setting alliances with the powerful local companies. The business partnering helps the multinational companies to wall against the increasingly winning competitors in the local marketplace and serving the stakeholders with the vision of "going global and acting local" with innovative and competitive differentiation. Such business expansion strategies have come true in the emerging markets, where multinational companies thrive to gain market leadership by building their brand image over the local products and services. In China and India, the instant food products, laundry detergent, and domestic appliance markets provide interesting examples of this phenomenon. The presence of multinational companies in the emerging markets has significantly affected the business of local enterprises. However, in some cases, foreign competitors have been able to resist the market gains of local competition, whether through first-mover advantages or by acquiring the leading local players and nurturing their local identity and strengths. Large companies in the local markets are able to make good returns by demonstrating the competitive differentiation by working continuously on the innovative projects and developing intangibles, such as product designs, technologies, management systems, and company cultures, partnering with local companies (Santos and Williamson 2015).

Competitive Differentiation

Companies have always bargained for competitive advantage in manufacturing and marketing of new innovative products, launching them with big infrastructure support, developing cost-effective strategies and combining it with competitive advantages, improving products and services efficiency, and managing customer-centric business operations to augment the stakeholders' value. One of the pertinent questions that drives the companies to ponder over is not "what more to make" but "how can the things be differentiated" to offer competitive advantage to the consumers. Such situation in the market has spurred because companies have poured identical and marginally differentiated products in the market that have strayed the consumer decisions and caused involuntary cannibalization of products within the product lines of a company. Thus, companies should establish clear and sustainable differentiation in their products and services, and work on innovative business projects to gain distinctive benefits in the competitive marketplace. The gravity of designing, developing, and carrying on innovative business projects demands to rethink of the conventional strategy principles from the perspective of the sources and locus of competitive advantage and cumulative advantage over the long term against the competitors in the marketplace. However, the market dynamics in the market today is driven by shifts in customers' purchase criteria rather than by improvements in products or technology (Dawar 2013).

Competition among firms in marketplace was regarded as a challenge toward developing and disseminating innovations among consumers in the 20th century, while it has become a way of doing business for firms in the 21st century. Firms emerge amidst competition, survive with the competing firms, and extinct or merge with stronger firms in the lifecycle. However, somewhat paradoxically, firms in a homogeneous marketplace survive with undifferentiated marketing strategies like selling identical products at the same price (Stigler 1957). International competition and the increasing globalization of business have driven global interest in the forms of governance for innovation-led production and differentiated marketing strategies. Potential firms evolve in the market competition through innovative manufacturing and marketing strategies, and developing a lean organization design. Competing firms embed their innovation insights in social networks to co-create value in business for sustainable growth.

Most consumer products manufacturing and marketing companies like Procter & Gamble (P&G) have driven its phenomenal growth over the past generation by innovating from within, successfully implementing many innovation projects and hiring the best talent across the destinations. Prior to globalization movement in the mid-20th century, most companies were smaller in their size of operation and were less competitive due to low involvement in innovative business projects. However, since 2000, a large number of companies have redefined their business growth objectives by spending greater amounts in innovation projects even for small returns as long as the innovative business project could set the percepts of competitive differentiation among consumers. Consumer products companies like P&G have replaced their conventional "invent within company" approach with an open "connect and develop" innovative business model to sustain market competition. By identifying innovation-led business projects and building on required capabilities and competencies to carry them on, P&G realized it could create better competitive differentiation and cheaper products faster by developing products faster and at relatively lower prices. Among most successful connect-and-develop products of P&G that made significant difference in the market are Olay Regenerist, Swiffer Dusters, the Crest Spin Brush, and the Mr. Clean Magic Eraser. Companies that are actively engaged in the innovation-led business models actively integrate suppliers, local manufacturers, and start-up entrepreneurs to work with new technologies, packages, and products that could create competitive differentiation in the marketplace. However, the low-resource companies are still adhering to conventional market infrastructure and are confined within the geo-demographic limits to carry out their innovation business insights (Hustin and Sakkab 2006).

A market within a competition scenario can be described at any specific point in time in terms of the direct and indirect connection among the market players (Cooke 1982). The market can, thus, be seen as a structure that is reconfigured as a result of strategic actions to outmaneuver and outperform competitors, and in this process, firms tend to switching suppliers, establishing new customer relationships, mergers and acquisitions, the formation or dissolution of strategic alliances, and forcing the entry or exit of sellers and buyers. Such strategic actions are major examples of firms reconfiguring the competitive strategy in an imperfect marketplace. The competition scenarios in the global marketplace through which firms pass in their lifecycle is as described as follows (Rajagopal 2014):

- Cocooning
- Open niche

- Expansion-industry competition
- Struggle for existence
- Survival of the fittest
- Consolidation
- Portfolio development
- Creating a posture
- Achieving sustainability in business

Small firms begin their business in a niche and try to achieve perfection in business by serving the consumer segment within the geo-demographic limits. Most firms initially monopolize their market with their innovative products in a niche and cocoon their marketing strategies blocking the entry of new firms in the niche. Operating on economies of scale for a large firm for commercializing the innovation-led products deliver competitive advantage significantly to the consumers at lower costs, which may further lead to the price leadership in the marketplace. In an open-market competition, there are different types and sizes of firms that use upfront marketing strategies and tactics to pull down the competing firms. Such competition forces small firms to struggle for existence against relatively large firms, while large firms strengthen their marketing strategies to sustain the competition and stay fittest in the competitive marketplace. However, large firms, at the early maturity stage of their business, attempt to consolidate their product line to stay abreast with market competition and develop product portfolio in tune to the market demand. In order to gain a suitable competitive position in the marketplace, firms pump enormous resources in innovation, technology, advertisement, communication, and sales activities. However, for some firms, returns on investment are not encouraging, and it builds sunk cost in the long run. The sunk costs are costs that have been incurred and cannot be reversed, such as spending on advertising or researching a product idea. They can be a barrier to entry. If potential entrants would have to incur similar costs, which would not be recoverable if the entry failed, they may be scared off. Another radical strategy may be used by the powerful firms to discourage entry by raising exit costs, for example, by making it an industry norm to hire workers on long-term contracts, which would build the escalated cost barriers for rival companies.

In the late maturity stage of firms in a competitive marketplace, firms engage resources in building corporate posture to sustain their business growth. A high corporate posture helps firms to stay sustainable in the competitive marketplace. Sustainable and high corporate posture builds trust among stakeholders of a firm and showcases the achievement of the organization's objectives in the market. The survival and success of a firm is a consequence of its capacity to establish competitive advantage and corporate reputation, and to maintain a relationship with its network of stakeholders.

As a number of firms are engaged in manufacturing and marketing of identical or similar products, the competition in the market manifolds. In such a competitive market scenario, large firms attempt to outperform small firms and acquire their market share. Large firms use high active pricing strategy by making higher investment in brand promotions and keeping the high price. Firms that have higher resources develop better customer relations for boosting customer loyalty than small firms, which have inadequate resources. Large firms cannibalize the market share of small firms also through mergers and acquisition, and building strategic alliance with other companies. On the contrary, smaller firms through consortium pose challenge to the large firms by adapting multiple market disruption strategies like low prices, disruptive innovation, mass marketing, and building customer loyalty at the bottom of the pyramid segments.

Competitive intelligence also contributes to the innovation learning process of a growing firm. Competitive intelligence is the information available to the competitors for free access on the public resources, which is periodically updated to present the current contents and potential strategic information. The information acquired by the competitors through public sources serves as an important input in formulating marketing strategy. A firm must be aware of the perspectives of its competitors before deciding which competitive moves to make. In order to acquire the required information on the competitions, firms must develop an internal fit with its employees, market players, and stakeholders. Mangers of the firm should determine information needs and should take the management of the firm to prepare for driving competitive intelligence. In acquiring competency on managing competitive intelligence, managers of the firm should look into the following perspectives (Rajagopal 2014):

- Developing an effective communication system within and outside the organizational system
- Knowing the competitor's organizational structure, culture, and environment
- Improving internal and external market analysis capabilities of firm
- Conducting an information resource gap-analysis
- Mapping competitor moves based on the competitive intelligence information review

Competitive intelligence includes information beyond industry statistics and trade gossip. It involves close observation of competitors to learn what they do best and why and where they are weak. There are three types of competitive intelligence—defensive, passive, and offensive. Defensive intelligence is the information gathered, analyzed, and used to avoid being caught off-balance. In this process, a deliberate attempt is made by the competing firm to gather information on the prevailing competition in a structured fashion, and to keep track of moves of the rivals that are relevant to the firm's business. Passive intelligence is the temporary information gathered for a specific decision. A company may, for example, seek information on a competitor's sales compensation plan when devising its own compensation plan. Offensive intelligence is the information gathered by the firms to identify new opportunities and from a strategic perspective. Such intelligence is most relevant for a growing firm amidst competition (Rajagopal 2012). Competitive intelligence is most commonly used by the following departments of a business firm:

- Innovation planning and research
- Research and development
- Business development
- Product planning
- Strategic planning
- Financial planning

A good competitive intelligence allows decision makers to prepare for changes in the market and act on the situation instead of reacting. Most firms engage external agencies to collect marketing information and competitor moves within the industry. Market research agencies collect information in a legal and ethical manner through valid primary, secondary, internal, and external sources. The competitive intelligence research agencies identify the patterns and anomalies in the acquired market information, and refine the data to support firms in developing appropriate competitive strategies and marketing decisions.

Firms operating in the global marketplace should know that there are two business scenarios that affect the management competitive intelligence. Firstly, environmental forces, which are external factors, such as events that can cause a company to achieve or fail to achieve its business objectives, and secondly, the competitive forces, which describe competitors' activities and plans (Pehrsson 2011).

Firms also maneuver the arena of customers, channels, institutions, and the geographical coverage in order to reconfigure their competitive strategy. The factor advantage in the competition may be defined as the relationship of the manufacturing or marketing company with the service providers who develop loyalty toward them. The service providers may be the suppliers of raw materials, packaging services, hiring of machines, and the like. Many companies use the legal support, government patronage, and so on to shape the competitive conditions to their advantage while building the institutional arena in the business. The software companies like Intel, Microsoft, and 3M always keep extending the product line, implementing the research and development results, and never let the competition stagnate in the end-customer arena. The healthy companies feel that greater the competition, higher will be the challenge to establish the brand in the market (Fahey 1999).

The conceptual framework of competitive forces in the marketplace has been provided by Porter as a five-force model for industry analysis comprising the interactivity of new entrants in the marketplace, availability of substitutes, bargaining power of suppliers and consumers as the key role players in marketing of products and services, and rivalry among the firms. These five forces of competition interact to determine the attractiveness of an industry. The economic value of a firm and brands thereof may be drained away among the existing competitors if the rivalry of firms within the industry is acute. However, it can also be bargained away through the power of suppliers or the power of customers, or be constrained by the threat of new entrants or the threat of substitutes. Competitive strategy can be viewed as building defenses against the competitive forces or as finding a position in an industry where the forces are weaker. The changes in the strength of the forces signal a change in the competitive landscape, which is often critical to ongoing strategy formulation (Porter 2008).

Innovation Trends

Consumers today are sensitive to the innovation and technology that offer sustainable competitive differentiation and deliver competitive stakeholder value. Most companies follow a boom-bust cycle in managing their innovation for improving business performance in the competitive marketplace. As companies rethink their priorities analyzing the market demand, they try to deliver innovation-led products and bring competitive differentiation against the existing and potential threats. Sustainable innovation requires a new approach to manage innovation initiatives, and companies need to build capabilities on improving the innovation processes. A network of innovation intermediaries including independent innovators and start-up companies would be visualizing new opportunities from the market insights and technologies to provide solutions to several companies. Such ideas might never occur to companies while working on their own (Wolpert 2002).

Innovation has emerged as a true engine of business growth for the companies after human capital. Innovative differentiation in the marketplace is brought in the markets by "start-up or seed companies" across the world, as it is evidenced by the big emerging markets like China and India in reference to the local growth and business dynamics. In order to maximize the business performance, companies should ensure that the key enablers of entrepreneurship and innovation, including managerial skills, capital, infrastructure, and research and development are applied to drive innovation. The innovation-driven companies should also overcome the challenges associated with asymmetric product demand and the changing consumer preferences. In short, innovation in a company needs to underpin any change faster than the competitors. Boosting innovation-led business performance largely depends on how quickly the company can move to competitive production that focuses on innovation and technology-driven products. Most companies are continuously engaged in bringing consumer innovations to the market, diffusing new insights among the market players to create quick impacts of competitive differentiations among the consumers. Gaining access to and deploying these innovations easily and cost-effectively in the market drives the success of companies today. The new technology trends in 21st century affect the innovation process of consumer-centric and business-to-business-oriented companies.

The Internet of Things (IoT), which has been termed by Cisco, refers to the "The Internet of Everything" and predicts that 50 billion devices (including our smartphones, appliances, and office equipment) will be wirelessly connected via a network of sensors to the Internet by 2020. Cisco also estimates that IoT will be valued at $4.6 trillion for the public sector in the next 10 years. These trends indicate that most companies that are engaged in innovation of consumer electronics, communication, geographic positioning devises, and information management systems would be relying on Internet-based technology as an integrated element. The key components of IoT include Big Data (and data mining), sensors (radio frequency identification, chips, semiconductors, and transistors), and business analytics giving predictive awareness to the companies about carrying out the innovative business projects. Companies engaged in IoT services innovations are focusing on facilities and infrastructure management, industrial applications, energy (smart grid), medical and health care, transportation, building or construction (smart buildings), environment (waste management), water resources, retail and supply chain, communications, and education (learning analytics). These companies use new technology trends toward automation, robotics, enabling nanotechnologies, self-assembling materials, artificial intelligence (AI) (human and computer interface), 3D printing photovoltaics and printed electronics), wearables (flexible electronics), real-time analytics and predictive analytics, supercomputing (faster and more connectivity), increased storage and data memory power, wireless networks, secure cloud computing, and virtualization. The trend of innovation today is focused largely on consumers and developing new markets for the industrial products as well. The attributes of innovation are exhibited in Figure 1.1.

The customer-centric innovations are growing rapidly in the global marketplace by assessing the needs and preferences of consumers and exploring the latent demand to determine the market potential, as illustrated in Figure 1.1. The consumer-centric innovation is carried out by the companies to deliver convenience, high perceived value in reference to application, satisfaction, and monetary gains in reference to the competitive differentiation. Consumer-led innovations are driven by the 4A-factors, comprising awareness, availability, affordability, and adaptability, reviewing the innovation lifecycle, sustainability, and scope to upgrade the technology embedded in the innovations. Industry-focused innovations are largely directed toward building new markets, acquiring new clients, achieving market leadership, and reinforcing corporate image in business-to-business market environment. Most of the innovative business projects are developed around the objectives of enhancing productivity with zero defects through lean manufacturing operations. Hence, most companies are employing automation using robotics-led

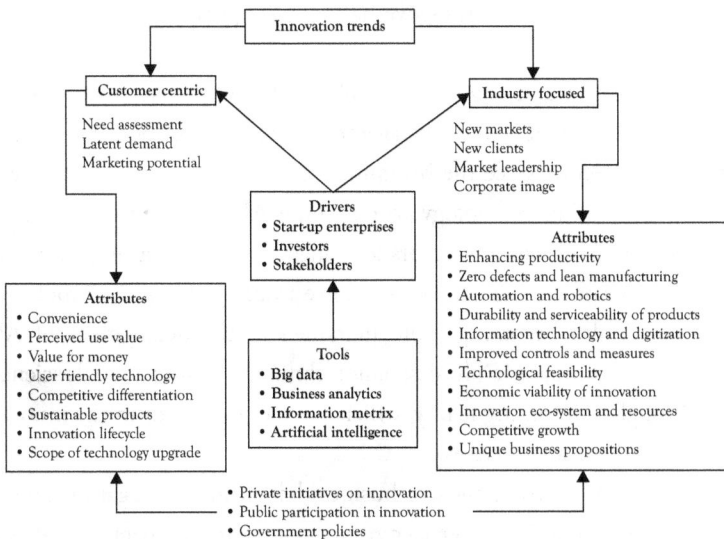

Figure 1.1 Trends and attributes of innovations

innovation and improved controls and measures. Industrial innovations have random growth in the marketplace driven by the emerging "start-ups" across the countries that offer new insights to the companies for their business growth. The upcoming "startups" extensively work with the information technology and offer digitization-led innovative solutions that offer competitive advantage and unique business proposition to the companies. However, for small startups, economic viability of the innovation appears to be an up-hill challenge.

Innovation and competitive insights among the companies are rapidly infiltrating since the early 21st century as the use of Big Data and business analytics has narrowed the information gap. The growing applications and advantages of information technology have been very supporting to the innovation of products and services, which helped the companies and public governance departments with the required tools to uncover trends, population movements, customer preferences, demographics, commerce traffic, transportation, and so on. These tools can also help several industries, including the customer service by identifying caller trends, health care by flagging potential fraud, and financial services by proactively flagging a borrower that is on the verge of lapsing in payment. The companies are innovating today within the digital transformation ambiance by digitizing the customer experience, managing data flow, cost-effective supply chain management, e-governance, and operating through virtual design centers.

Emergent AI and augmented reality technologies are rapidly being applied in the services and management operations in both the public and private sectors since the beginning of 21st century. Companies are already developing technology to distribute AI software to millions of graphics and computer processors to manage machine learning, and natural language processing that helps to solve a variety of business problems. Robotics is also becoming more ingrained in the deployment of AI. Recent breakthroughs in physics, nanotechnologies, and materials science have brought computing reality, which has set new trends in the innovation of products and services.

One of the recent trends in business has been extravagantly driven by the innovating consumer electronics with remote operating devises among the companies across the destinations in the world. The new innovations are built around the amateur brands in the market manu-factured by the start-up companies or niche companies and marketed by online outlets including Amazon.com and many regional virtual out-lets. The performance of such new innovations is widely discussed on social media and consumer networks anchored by the popular blogs and online discussion forums. Sharing of verbal (text) and nonverbal (video) consumer generated contents has emerged as the most powerful busi-ness performance tool. Attentive start-up entrepreneurs have introduced the Instagram application by motivating instant art-photographers who could brainstorm on social media by asking perception and experience of consumers about new of brands products and services of the companies.

Most of the innovations triggered by the SUEs are woven around consumer needs and their preferences toward convenience, sustainable technology, and value for money bargain. Such product innovations include technology-driven products for the mass consumers. Robotic tech-nology with easy-to-use baby products, such as a baby seat that bounces and sways like human parents, has emerged as a crash performer in the United States, while some innovation are also marketed for meeting social responsibility. For example, an emerging company Boll and Branch in Chatham, NJ, has developed organic, fair-trade, and direct-to-consumer bedding, and dedicated a portion of the revenue earned from the sales of this project to "Not for Sale," an antihuman-trafficking organization. Another innovation in consumer foods is about nongenetically modified food carried out in a nonconventional way. An engineer by training, who spent months perfecting the recipe for coconut chips, which he needed for his mother's Thai lettuce wraps, worked on innovative coconut chips with five flavors from Salted Caramel to Original. He developed a fam-ily business to export his innovative snacks from Thailand. In 2014, his products won "The Best Snack Award" in the Fancy Foods Show, in the United States, and in 2012, the entrepreneur built a non-GMO certified company known as Dang Foods in Berkley, CA, with the exclusivity of his innovation. Such business projects originate from the startups and grow as companies, provided the innovations are nurtured properly during the business-evolution process.

Another "startup" way of innovation-led marketing strategy can be cited of "Ringly," an upcoming company in New York City, which combined technology and high fashion to stay connected in a discreet and stylish way in the competitive marketplace. Ringly started with a boom by selling over 1,000 rings in their first 24 hours of business. They are now working to create new additions to their jewelry collection and to develop partnerships with different fashion brands. The former eBay product manager teamed up with other engineers from Stanford, MIT, and Carnegie Mellon University to develop a stylish solution in mid-2013. This company could raise notable funds within short time and could successfully rope-in big investors like Andreessen Horowitz, Silas Capital, and First Round Capital. A conventional insight with modern approach has been coined by three young start-up entrepreneurs who raised a company "Blue Apron" in New York City, NY, with the distribution of farm-fresh ingredients along with the innovative recipes awaking a chef in every consumer.

Innovation is a continuous process, whether in consumer products or industrial goods. Laundry detergent has a chronological evolution of innovation and has gained quick first-mover advantages by transforming the consumer preferences accordingly. The transformation has occurred along many dimensions from hard bar soap, to flakes, to powder, and to liquid over the period. The innovation in the product also distinguished the product attributes from animal fats and vegetable oils to synthetic nonsoap detergents by augmenting the use in high-efficiency washing machines and quality of water, including temperature preferences of hot and cold water. On the green business innovation front, the idea of solar charger consumer electronics has grown the market demand. The Window Solar Charger brought out in the market by several competing niche-led companies can be used to power your smartphone through sunlight from the window. The charger is a rechargeable lithium battery that holds 1400 mAh of electric charge. This device delivers completely green energy, as it is all collected through solar panels on the window-facing side of the device.

Innovative Business Projects: Lessons Learned

In the mid-20th century, the need for innovations in the retail and industrial business has emerged as a pertinent need to drive the business performance and growth. Companies accordingly engaged in identifying the need for innovation, by exploring opportunities to develop innovation with competitive differentiation, build organizational capability and competence to manage innovation process, and allocate resources for carrying out innovation. Most companies wanted their product development teams to create breakthroughs by developing and launching new products that would allow their companies to grow rapidly and maintain high margins. However, exploring innovations for breakthroughs has been expensive and time-consuming for the companies when carried out fully within the organization, as innovators, product developers, and process manager often got lost in the process of achieving breakthroughs due to unclear system within the company to guide innovation. By the mid-1990s, the lack of such system was a problem even for an innovative company like 3M, when it was engaged in developing breakthrough products and the lead-user process. The lead-user process was intended to transforms the task of inventing breakthroughs into a systematic task of identifying the lead users and learning from them (von Hippel, Thomke, and Sonnack 1999). The two common ways of developing and managing innovative business projects have later emerged within and outside of the corporate environment. Most companies consider innovation as a continuous process and invest resources in business innovation projects. However, low-capital innovative business projects are run by the SUEs, who develop the innovation concepts, prototypes, and business plan for large-scale implementation, and look for potential companies to adopt the innovative business project for implementing to scales. The co-creation of innovation and managing innovative business project at various organizational levels have set new trends in the global business environment.

In the new innovation ambiance, companies and startups realize that they have to coexist and identify new ways to influence each other for managing innovative business projects and segment performance. This experience paved the way for the get-into-business stage, in which SUEs and large companies could manage successful businesses. In the process, SUEs learned business discipline from the private sector, while corporations gained innovative insights to lead the marketplace. Increased success on both sides has laid the foundation the co-creating the innovation, in which companies deliver high value to stakeholders. Alternatively, nongovernment organizations (NGO) also actively collaborate with the companies in diffusing the innovation. When Bharat Petroleum (BP) sought to market a dual-fuel portable stove in India, it set up one such co-creation system with three Indian NGOs. The system allowed BP to bring the innovative stove to a geographically dispersed market through numerous local distributors. While the company sold its stoves profitably, the NGOs gained access to a lucrative revenue stream that could fund other innovative business projects (Prahalad and Brugmann 2007).

Companies that are working on innovative projects carry a set of risks. In most large firms, employees are constantly stormed with ideas for new projects, and most often, there exists resistance within the organization. And even if new ideas get the support from the top management, the innovative business projects face many challenges toward their implementation, including finding sponsors, building innovation prototypes to the scale of production, managing capital and resources; and developing competitive advantage of innovation in the market and creating the stakeholder value (Miller and Wedellsborg 2013). The sources of innovation are getting more dispersed geo-demographically as well as industry-wise, and objectives in carrying innovation have shifted from technology to business models. Many innovations now come from simplifying or scaling down the existing products or services and fragmenting the earlier structure of products. Hence, companies should align their innovation plans with the business strategies that could deliver unique competitive advantages and manage stakeholder values. In the past, companies were focused on applying technology to innovate their products and services; however, many firms have recently started to actively license out technology. These firms consider technology licensing for umbrella production of the innovative products simultaneously at various destinations in collaboration with partnering companies for commercializing the innovation rapidly across the markets. The current trends of innovation and organizational approaches toward managing innovations in the global marketplace are exhibited in Figure 1.2.

Most companies are also engaging consumers in the innovation process and learning from their experience in the past with similar products of other companies. Such trend of bottom-up innovation is largely

| Start-up initiatives
Collaboration with sponsors
Managing innovation
Innovation upgrades
Open innovation | | | Innovation alliances
Business alliances
Kaizen approach
Start-up enterprises |

| Innovation within organization | Outsourcing innovation | Public-private innovation | Collaborative innovation |

| Identifying needs
Building capability and competence
Allocating resources
Innovation sponsor | | Crowdsourcing ideas
Nongovernmental organizations
Experience innovation
Consumer engagement | |

Innovation trends in global marketplace

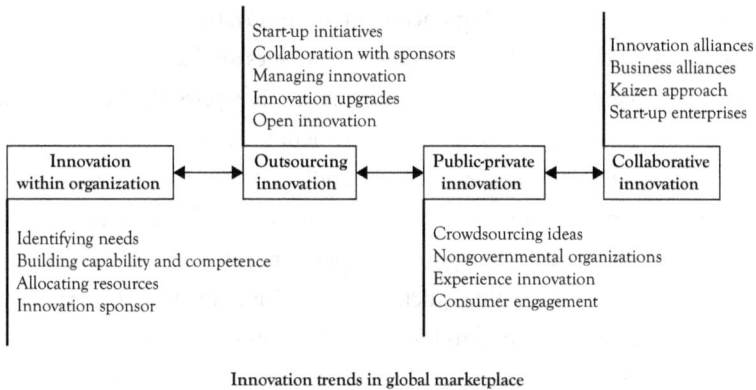

Figure 1.2 Innovation trends and organizational approaches

anchored by social network groups connected with the companies as illustrated in Figure 1.2 in reference to public-private innovation, engaging consumers in the innovation process by sharing new ideas and concepts based on their experience. Such experience-led innovations are largely adopted from the societal trends, and innovation concepts are developed for experimentation. Customer-centric companies, such as LEGO, Starbucks Coffee, and Fab India, believe in innovation by creating value creation that will shift the business culture from products and services to experience environments and co-creation of innovations. The experience innovations carried out in the companies not only improve the product or service, but also enable the need-based co-creation of an environment in which personalized, evolvable innovation can be nurtured. The success of customer-centric innovations grows out of individual consumers co-creating their own unique value, and consumer communities on the digital platform support the companies to appropriately diffuse the innovation across the consumer segments. Over the period, consumer networks, social communication, and adaptive learning are fostering experience innovation in the multinational companies, such as Sony, Apple, Microsoft, and TiVo, illustrating the budding trend toward experience innovation (Prahalad and Ramaswamy 2003).

As most companies are continuously engaged in innovations in the global marketplace, there appears to be escalation in the research and development costs and increase in the risk of commercializing the innovations.

Hence, companies are facing uncertainty in innovation adaptation, causing decrease in the product revenues. Companies are facing such risk also due to frequent innovations driving product lifecycles shorter. Though companies are deploying manifold investment toward innovations to gain competitive differentiations, they are finding it increasingly difficult to justify investments in innovation due to embedded risk and uncertainties. Hence, companies are leaning toward open innovation that balances lowering the risk and generating quick returns on investment on innovations. The open innovations tend to lower the development costs of innovation by the greater use of external technology in carrying out the research and development activities. This saves time as well as money, and the firm no longer restricts itself to the markets it serves directly. Open innovation is an emerging model in which companies invite innovation ideas from crowdsourcing and use external ideas, screen them from the point of view of economic viability and technological feasibility of adopting the new ideas. Simultaneously, companies also encourage employees to share ideas within the company or industry group and determine the internal and external paths to market. Open innovation is based on co-created platforms of architectures and systems by the various market players, including consumers, distributors, retailers, and technology experts, who set the innovation requirements and develop an appropriate business model.

Another upcoming trend shows that companies develop collaborative business innovation projects with other companies or SUEs by paying the licensing fee for the innovation adoption or developing joint ventures with the partnering company in innovation over the long term. By working on such terms of reference, companies co-create and nurture innovations with their business partners and ensure substantial revenue from the innovation. In order to derive the benefits of open innovation, companies augment their ability to experiment with new business models and finding ways to work with them (Chesbrough 2007). Building innovation capability in a company requires employing the experimentation process for continuous improvement (Kaizen), conducting experiments and assessing their results to improve the business performance within the company and in collaboration with the partnering firms. Kaizen is the practice of continuous improvement, which was originally introduced to the global marketplace by Japanese companies. Today, Kaizen is recognized worldwide as an important pillar of an organization's long-term competitive strategy. Kaizen also supports the open innovation business models, and most companies use Kaizen as a tool for sourcing innovation ideas. Companies commercialize selectively the open ideas by deploying pathways to bring the innovation to the market, while internal ideas are processed through channels outside of their current businesses in order to generate value for the stakeholders as well as to build competitive differentiation of the company.

Critical Success Factors

Successful innovation leads to customer involvement and profits, which can be achieved through the co-creation by aligning consumers and market players in the innovation process. Some multinational companies have invested resources, taking advantage of social media to diffuse new ideas and stimulating co-creation of innovative products and services. For many companies, developing innovative products does not occur as a chance or coincidence, but through careful attention to many important criteria. Firms should analyze their innovation practices and capabilities to become more effective in driving innovation as breakthrough and gain competitive advantage. The contribution of employees toward innovation in products, services, or strategy signifies the value and quality of innovation portfolio of an organization, and projects the innovation-effectiveness curve of the company. Breakthrough innovations in markets are a continuous process, which is backed by the distribution, retailing, and services industry. Innovations leading to commercial breakthroughs demonstrate a highly skewed distribution of the use value of inventions, explaining that some are useless, a few are of moderate value, and there is rarely one that qualifies as a breakthrough. Those breakthroughs embed the long tail of innovation, and distribution plays a key role in the breakthrough process. It is necessary for the firms to account for the total number of inventions a company generates, the average score out of the mean value of those inventions, and to count the number of successful breakthrough inventions.

Successful innovation of new products leads to customer engagement and profits. Some companies have tried investing intensively in research and development. For many companies, developing new products is a hit-or-miss the market task, but successful innovation is not magical. It comes from careful attention to a small number of important criteria. The key question is not how much a company can spend, but the ways to spend money in the innovation process. The return on innovation investment concept correlates directly with the organic growth, and links innovation spending with the financial performance in ways that can lead decision makers to generate higher, more reliable returns on innovation, and research and development. Successful innovations are sustainable in the market if developed with a better understanding of marketing metrics and the way managers use them. Indeed, doing so will enforce the application of accurate metrics that are capable of measuring the financial and nonfinancial impacts of innovation and marketing decisions. Considering that innovation investment decisions involve all product development and marketing divisions and often have a strategic impact within the company, understanding the return on investment for an innovation is assured. Often managers of multitask innovation companies are typically confronted with the need to justify their investments on innovations, defend prospective projects, and measure past and future expenses and outcomes.

It is necessary for the companies to build appropriate innovation ecosystems to carry out the innovation business projects successfully. Leveraging tasks within the predetermined innovation ecosystem reduces various risks related to the manufacturing, project process, and commercialization. Random innovations are characterized by the fundamental types of risk that encompass innovation initiative risks, which are the familiar uncertainties of managing a project, interdependence risks comprising uncertainties of coordinating with alliance or outsourced innovators or SUEs, and integration risks causing the uncertainties occurring during the adoption process across the innovation value chain. Firms that work within the innovation ecosystem and could assess risks holistically in an innovative business project and systematically establish realistic expectations, develop a more refined set of environmental contingencies, and arrive at a more robust innovation strategy could make the innovation successful (Adner 2006).

In order to ensure success in commercializing innovation, companies need to invest substantially in the innovative business projects and allocate resources to manage the innovation process at various stages of the project. Lack of resources, or midterm withdrawals of the innovation projects lead to desertion of the innovation and have low effect on commercialization. Innovation success rates are typically low, and returns are slow if they frequently reverse the innovation at various stages of the innovation path, that also escalates the cost, time, and effect of the commercializing an innovation. This makes innovation initiatives hard to justify when resources are limited and company has inadequate competence in carrying out the innovations. Companies intending to carry out innovations and commercialize them in the marketplace should include the following critical success factors:

- Understanding the consumer needs and consumption patterns appropriately
- Exploring the opportunities for innovation within and outside the organization
- Identifying a compelling innovation business project and setting its development path
- Scope of sustainability of the innovation in future
- Delineating the innovation agenda and developing a stages and review (stage-gate) process
- Ensuring employee involvement, including the top-management executives
- Develop a decision model to carry out innovation in teams and integrate the sectional growth of innovation carried out by different teams
- Building capability and competence in the multifunctional teams carrying out innovations
- Exploring marketplace drivers for managing innovation
- Risk absorption and contingency plan during the innovation and commercialization process
- Elaborative execution plan, including concept testing, market testing, services support, and creating customer value

Innovations can be successfully commercialized by the companies, provided consumers understand why the innovation is necessary. Thus, companies need to diffuse extensively the prototype experience among consumers and generate awareness about the competitive differentiation of the innovation. Failing to create an appropriate marketplace environment for the innovation, companies might lose the business on innovation or the performance in the battle for resources. The performance engine of innovation is bigger, central to the market power, and can reveal the business outcome based on the strategies of the company. So, the case for innovation has to be made only when it is compelling for the company from the point of commercialization and market responsiveness. Companies should take up innovation projects that have minimum three-year market span with the current generation attributes and may assure market for over 10 years with consecutive generations. For example, *iPhone* of Apple Inc. and *Galaxy* series mobile phones by Samsung have innovations over generations and are keeping their marketing share growing in the global marketplace. Before preparing the innovation development agenda, setting stages and review gates, and mapping the innovation path, companies should essentially find response to the questions on how a specific innovation supports the business, and what are the admissible risk tolerance and contingency plans for recovering the business. Companies with clear innovation strategies, decision metrics, and sustainability of innovation push the incremental innovation projects in the marketplace. Breakthrough innovations can survive if the companies have a sustainable decision-making model that is different from the one used for incremental spread over a series of small improvements or upgrades made to a company's existing products, services, processes, or methods. In order to carry out innovations successfully, companies should promote team culture. The best teams' project champions, who can make appropriate decisions, get sponsors and develop relevant capabilities and expertise to carry on the innovation process (Govindarajan 2011).

Product innovation is a systematic process, and it needs to be carried out with a fully aligned agenda mapping the tasks, causes, and effects. The development of a new product would not be successful if activities in all stages are not properly networked. A stage-gate model should be followed in carrying out the product innovation process to minimize the risk of failure. This model depicts a conceptual and operational roadmap for moving a new product project from an idea to the launch. This model divides the effort into distinct stages separated by management decision gates. Cross-functional teams must successfully complete a prescribed set of related cross-functional tasks in each stage prior to obtaining management approval to proceed to the next stage of product development. Stage-gate processes have a great deal of appeal to management, because, basically, they restrict investment in the next stage until management is comfortable with the outcome of the current stage. The gate can be effective in controlling product quality and development expense. Stages and gates in the model function as sequential phases and may run into some overlapping activities, especially when they cross the decision points. The stage-gate processes may not lead toward completing tasks in earlier phases to keep them off of the critical path, but they foster a mindset in which the work proceeds sequentially step by step. A newer alternative to the stage-gate process is the bounding box approach, which is essentially a management by exceptions technique, in which certain critical parameters of the project, such as profit margin, project budget, product performance level, and launch date, are negotiated as the bounding box. Firms need to conduct regular checks, so that the process managers remain within bounds (Rajagopal 2012). The stage-gate process begins with the identification and documentation of a new idea in improving business. Tasks associated with the development of the product are then divided into a sequence of logical steps called *stages*, each of which is preceded by a *gate* where the attractiveness of the project is assessed. During each stage, a cross-functional project team carries out tasks that result in the completion of defined deliverables, including those related to technological (manufacturing, research and development, quality, and regulatory) and business (sales, marketing, and business development) functions.

A disciplined, managed approach to innovation can make the innovation process more predictable, repeatable, and profitable, leading to better top- and bottom-line results and overall high performance. While many firms believe that innovation is a creative endeavor that cannot be managed, the fact is that an effective innovation requires cross-functional cooperation and accountability throughout the entire process. No innovation is a one-size-fits-all endeavor, and organizations may need to deploy multiple processes, one for breakthrough-type innovations and another for line extension-type based on the improvements in the existing products within the product line. Successful innovators have a portfolio of innovations in the pipeline, ranging from modest line extensions to bigger bets on new ideas or technologies. However, it is wise to keep shorter portfolios and focus on both low and high risk ideas in reference to target markets, where innovative products are set to be launched. Accordingly, companies may manipulate product lifecycles and influence the evolving consumer demands to support innovation. Social media tools should also have the potential to accelerate innovation at all phases of development, from ideation to prototype development to pilot programs to commercialization. The critical success factors of an innovation-led product in the competitive marketplace are associated with the following constituents:

- Identifying the right need for product innovation at the right time
- Projecting the scope of new products in reference to the elapse time between the stages of the innovation lifecycle
- Properly aligning and networking all activities in the product-innovation process
- Involving the senior management of the company at each phase of the innovation process
- Encouraging cross-functional teamwork and effective organizational leadership to carry the product innovation
- Driving a prochange learning attitude among the employees, so that flexible thinking on product innovation may be inculcated to develop an end-user-centric product

Any roaming idea might not seed an innovation. Firms should find rationale to a good reason to nurture an idea to carry out organizational level innovations that may motivate a sustainable business growth. Unless managers understand why innovation is necessary, it always leaps off the core business and drains resources without yielding desired returns. In order to sustain the innovation on the performance parameters of tactical and strategic returns on investment, managers should be able to make the case for product innovation indeed compelling. It is important for the product innovators to foresee the growth and sustainability of innovation measuring the probable elapsed time between the stages of innovation lifecycle. Though history market and consumer behavior of similar or identical products set the future prospects of innovation-led products, firms should recognize tidal forces of anticipated change in the market for the new products and associated services.

Incremental innovation can be integrated into the organizational learning process with clear strategy, rightly placed and measured decision metrics, and management models like stage-gate to create a working platform for all those involved in the innovation process. It is, thus, necessary to involve also the senior management of the firm to run the innovation process through the stage-gate paradigm and review the performance of activities at each stage to open the gate to carry innovation to the next stage. The innovation process is a teamwork, as it involves various functionaries to coordinate at different levels to let the innovative product into the market. Autocratic decision making fails to engage all players in the product-innovation process, including critical stakeholders, while a consensus not based on the rationale sinks every decision to its lowest possible effect. The innovation process does not function without a leadership who can make decisions and engage the team to support those decisions. Companies should develop cross-functional teams to drive steering of insights and mutual responsiveness in performing various operational tasks. The best teams have five critical dimensions that comprise warming, forming, storming, norming, and performing (Rajagopal 2014).

In practice, today's global competition is more dynamic and multidimensional. The mature industry paradox is that leadership demands differentiation, yet differences are quickly copied. Single-factor innovations tap one competency, and capable competitors can usually match it. Multiple competencies strengthen several dimensions, and in effect, redefine the basis of competition. The "shadow strategy task force" is offered as a method to force managers to relinquish the comfort of the firm's accepted view of itself. This approach begins with the objective of identifying the strategies and competency that, in the hands of competitors, might be used to attack the firm's competitive position successfully. Especially critical on the task force are individuals with insight into how customers, suppliers, and competitors view the firm's products and services. Developing new competency requires constant experimentation. The innovation-imitation-equilibrium cycle suggests that industry leaders teach customers what to demand by defining the current state-of-the-art in performance, price, service, and other dimensions; customers learn to judge competitive offerings against these standards, and the learning effect is cumulative (Werther and Kerr 1995).

There are many ways to categorize the core competencies by developing market-access competency, integrity-related competency, and functionality-related competency. The market-access competency includes the management of brand development, sales and marketing, distribution and logistics, technical support, and so on. All these skills help to put a firm in close proximity to its customers. The attributes associated with competency like quality, cycle time management, just-in-time inventory management, and so on, which allow a company to do things more quickly, flexibly, or with a higher degree of reliability than competitors, constitute the integrity-related competency of a firm. The functionality-related competency leads to the skills that enable the company to invest its services or products with unique functionality and invest the product with distinctive customer benefits, rather than merely making it incrementally better. The functionality-related competency is becoming more important as a source of competitive differentiation, relative to the other two types of competencies. In the growing competitive phenomenon, the companies are converging toward universally high standards for product and service integrity, and are moving through alliances, acquisitions, and industry consolidation to build broadly matching global brand and distribution capabilities. Interestingly, the Japanese concept of quality has shifted from an idea centered on integrity ("zero defects") to one focused on functionality ("quality that surprises" in that the product yields a unique functionality benefit to the customer). Comparative analysis examines the specific advantages of competitors within a given market and offers structural and response advantages. Structural advantages are those built into the business for example, a manufacturing plant in Mexico may, because of low labor costs, have a built-in advantage over another firms. Responsive advantages refer to the positions of comparative advantage that have accrued to a business over time as a result of certain decisions. This type of advantage is based on leveraging the strategic phenomena at work in the business. Besides, the examination of the business system operating in an industry is useful in analyzing competitors and in searching out innovative options for gaining a sustainable competitive advantage. The business-system framework enables a firm to discover the sources of greatest economic leverage, that is, stages in the system where it may build cost or investment barriers against competitors (Norman and Ramirez 1993).

Innovations in Emerging Markets

Innovations in the emerging markets are sprouting through the manifold growth of SUEs that are sponsored by the large companies in various fields, from consumer electronics to e-commerce and community health to sustainability of product and services. Innovations in the emerging markets are carried on in both business-to-consumer and business-to-business segments that are being nurtured by the sponsoring companies to facilitate the innovation to commercialize and gain quick returns on innovations. The small start-up entrepreneurs in the emerging markets are working on the low-cost and sustainable innovations that deliver desirable results and enhance the perceived use value of the consumers. Accordingly, reverse innovation is pacing fast in the emerging markets, giving a major competitive challenge to the companies intending to penetrate high technology, high cost innovative product in the marketplace. As the emerging markets are responding faster to innovation and technology, the gap between premier and mass or bottom-of-the-pyramid is narrowing down. As a result, the global dynamics of innovation are changing. No longer will innovations navigate the globe in the top-down consumer segments direction, in the emerging markets, they are also flowing in reverse. Reverse innovation guides the managers of the sponsor companies how to make innovation in the emerging markets happen and how such innovations can unlock opportunities in the global marketplace. Reverse innovation has become a think-tank of innovative ideas in the emerging markets and drifting them to flow uphill to markets in Europe and North America. Such trend has thrown immense challenges in the business community as it demands a company to overcome the institutionalized thinking that guides its actions toward managing innovative projects within the organization.

The growth of innovations in the emerging markets and the process of their commercialization has been exhibited in Figure 1.3.

The ecosystem of innovation in emerging markets is built around the consumer needs, SUEs, innovation gateways comprising sponsorship, co-creation, open innovation, and reverse innovation, as exhibited in the Figure 1.3. Most innovations are grown in the emerging markets around the ethnic needs of consumers and developed at low cost considering the affordability and adaptability potentials of the consumers in the home market. Often such innovations developed for niche markets are commercialized by the large companies and are modified to fit into the extended geo-demographic market segments. Accordingly, the companies sponsoring the innovation initiatives with SUEs in the emerging markets build capability and competence among the SUEs and determine the lifecycle of innovative products by evaluating the value-for-money consumer perception of these products. The routes to market an innovative product refer to the channels, such as brick-and-mortar stores, online stores, M-commerce outlets, and direct marketing (one-on-one), that help the companies to diffuse innovation in the market as well as to develop consumer outreach to the innovative products. The companies that are engaged in commercializing innovations, either acquired from

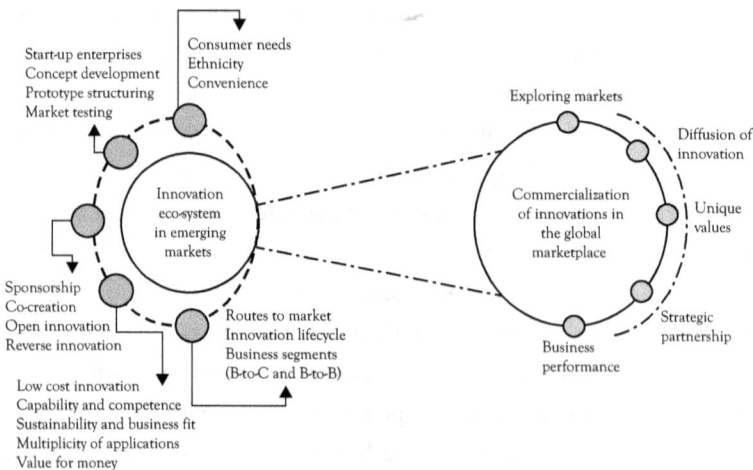

Figure 1.3 **Innovation ecosystem in the emerging markets and commercialization**

SUEs or co-created, invest enormous resources in exploring markets for launching innovations, carrying out diffusion of innovation, and creating unique values of innovation by exhibiting competitive differentiation and advantages to the consumers. Successful SUEs in the emerging markets develop strategic partnership with the sponsors or large companies to launch and manage incremental innovations in the competitive marketplace. Such strategic partnerships serve the business-to-consumer and business-to-business market segments in the destination markets.

Most consumer-led innovations have been carried out using the informational technology resources. IT-based innovations are largely developed in emerging markets by the SUEs and shared with the companies for improving their business performance. For example, Eat2Eat.com was an Internet-based restaurant reservation service, covering a dozen cities in the Asia-Pacific region developed by an entrepreneur and former investment banker with USD 1 million of his own capital. The Singapore-based Eat2Eat Pvt. Ltd. has launched this online service facilitating application, an IT-based innovation in 2000 after quickly establishing the capabilities and business model in association with the SUE. Initially, this application received low response and over five years, the registered user base remained relatively small at about 12,000. In the next phase, the company had expanded that user base and hoped that the company could change the way people made plans to eat out. Alike most start-up innovation business projects in the emerging markets, resources in reference to time and money in carrying out this innovative application were limited. Consequently, offering adequate sales and promotions to commercialize the Eat2Eat web-based application had been a challenge to the company (Hardy and Goodwin 2006). Another example can be cited of a small Israeli startup TaKaDu, which had developed an innovative software system that used patented algorithms and statistical analysis to detect problems such as leaks, bursts, and faulty equipment within a water utility's infrastructure. Such problems caused significant water and energy loss at many utilities, led to service interruptions for consumers, and were only getting worse as the existing infrastructure aged (Ofek and Preble 2013).

Multinational companies are leaning toward the logic of reverse innovation, in which products are designed first for consumers in low-income countries and then adapted into disruptive offerings for developed economies. In this process, the emerging markets play as key drivers and serve as innovation routers. However, only a handful of companies have managed to do it successfully until now. Multinational companies with capital-intensive innovation process, which get the products developed through western designers following time-tested methods, struggle to overcome the constraints and leverage the consumerism of the emerging markets. Managing reverse innovations for large companies hailing from developed countries appears to difficult in reference to matching segments to the existing products, lowering price by removing features, failing to think through all the technical requirements, neglecting stakeholders, and refusing to believe products created for low-income markets that could also have a global appeal. But, companies can avoid these traps by defining the problems independently beyond innovation, reducing the overriding features in the innovative products and improving the functionality. To do so, the companies use the best-available solutions in the emerging markets that could help in lowering the price, analyze technological landscape that could fit into the requirements of the emerging markets, and analyze the value perceptions of stakeholders.

Innovation and technology in consumer and business-to-business products in the global marketplace are growing fast to gain strategic and tactical competitive advantages. Almost every advance in innovation and technology in the consumer products segment is emerging as a breakthrough, and the opportunities for the next generation grow ever longer. Though every emerging technology will change the business or social platforms, only some sustain with the potential to grow generically or disrupt the existing commercial innovation products, service, or technologies. The new technologies and innovative products help in transforming lives of people and work ambience, and rearrange value pools beyond business benefits. It is, therefore, critical that business and policy leaders understand which technologies will matter to them and prepare accordingly. In order to cope-up with the advancing innovation and technology developments in the global marketplace, potential companies should stay on-guards in the market and keep their organizational strategies updated for converging marketing policies with the shifting consumer demand. Business leaders should ensure that organizations continue to look ahead, and drive user-friendly innovation and technologies to improve internal performance as well. However, organizations should also measure the lifecycle of new innovations and technologies, and assess the possibility of penetration of disruptive technologies in the market that could shorten the predetermined lifecycle of innovative- and technology-led products. Disruptive technologies can change the game for businesses, creating entirely new products and services as well as shifting pools of value between producers or from producers to consumers. Organizations will often need to use business model innovations to capture some of that value and drive managers to consider various scenarios to develop a sustainable innovation and technology plan. However, firms may take all precautions while abandoning or undermining assumptions about the threat of market competition and risk to develop strategic business models. In the growing technology market scenario, the emerging market companies will turn as significant competitors and thrive to enhance profit from new technology applications as they become available. The emerging markets will create plenty of opportunities related to smart technology, and they will not be limited to for-profit enterprises.

References

Adner, R. 2006. "Match Your Innovation Strategy to Your Innovation Ecosystem." *Harvard Business Review* 83, no. 4, pp. 98–116.

Cavusgil, S.T., and G. Knight. 2009. *Born Global Firms: A New International Enterprise*. New York, NY: Business Expert Press.

Chesbrough, H.W. 2007. "Why Companies Should Have Open Business Models." *MIT Sloan Management Review* 48, no. 2, pp. 22–28.

Cooke, P. 1982. "Dependency, Supply Factors and Uneven Development in Wales and Other Problem Regions, Regional Studies." *The Journal of the Regional Studies Association* 16, no. 3, pp. 211–27.

Dawar, N. 2013. "When Marketing is Strategy." *Harvard Business Review* 91, no. 12, pp. 100–8.

Fahey, L. 1999. *Competitors: Outwitting, Outmaneuvering and Outperforming*. Canada: John Wiley and Sons.

Govindarajan, V. July 5, 2011. "Innovation's Nine Critical Success Factors." HBR Blog Network. Retrieved on September 03, 2013 from http://blogs.hbr.org/govindarajan/2011/07/innovations-9-critical-success.html

Hardy, K.G., and N. Goodwin. 2006. *Eat2Eat.com*. Cambridge, MA: Harvard Business School Press.

Hustin, L., and N. Sakkab. 2006. "Connect and Develop: Inside Procter and Gamble's New Model for Innovation." *Harvard Business Review* 84, no. 3, pp. 58–66.

Michel, S. 2014. "Capture More Value." *Harvard Business Review* 92, no. 10, pp. 78–85.

Miller, P., and T.W. Wedellsborg. 2013. "The Case for Stealth Innovation." *Harvard Business Review* 91, no. 3, pp. 90–97.

Normann, R., and R. Ramirez. 1993. "From Value Chain to Value Constellation-Designing Interactive Strategy." *Harvard Business Review* 71, no. 4, pp. 65–77.

Ofek, O., and M. Preble. 2013. *TaKaDu*. Cambridge, MA: Harvard Business School Press.

Pehrsson, A. 2011. "Product/Customer Scope: Competition Antecedents, Performance Effects and Market Context Moderations." *European Business Review* 23, no. 5, pp. 418–33.

Porter, M.E. 2008. "The Five Competitive Forces that Shape Strategy." *Harvard Business Review* 68, no. 3, pp. 79–93.

Prahalad, C.K., and J. Brugmann. 2007. "Cocreating Business's New Social Compact." *Harvard Business Review* 85, no. 2, pp. 80–90.

Prahalad, C.K., and V. Ramaswamy. 2003. "New Frontier of Experience Innovation." *MIT Sloan Management Review* 44, no. 4, pp. 12–18.

Rajagopal. 2012. *Systems Thinking and Process Dynamics for Marketing Systems: Technologies and Applications for Decision Management*. Hershey, PA: IGI Global.

Rajagopal. 2014. *Architecting Enterprise: Managing Innovation, Technology, and Global Competitiveness*. Basingstoke, NH: Palgrave Macmillan.

Santos, J.F.P., and P.J. Williamson. 2015. "The New Mission for Multinationals." *MIT Sloan Management Review* 56, no. 4, pp. 45–54.

Stigler, G.J. 1957. "Perfect Competition, Historically Contemplated." *Journal of Political Economy* 65, no. 1, pp. 1–17.

Svensson, G. 2002. "Beyond Global Marketing and the Globalization of Marketing Activities." *Management Decision* 40, no. 6, pp. 574–83.

von Hippel, E., S. Thomke, and M. Sonnack. 1999. "Creating Breakthroughs at 3 M." *Harvard Business Review* 77, no. 5, pp. 47–55.

Werther, W.B., and J.L. Kerr. 1995. "The Shifting Sands of Competitive Advantage." *Business Horizons* 38, no. 3, pp. 11–17.

Wolpert, J.D. 2002. "Breaking Out of the Innovation Box." *Harvard Business Review* 80, no. 8, pp. 76–83.

Yoder, S., J.K. Visich, and E. Rustambekov. 2016. "Lessons Learned from International Expansion Failures and Successes." *Business Horizons* 59, no. 2, pp. 233–43.

CHAPTER 2

Analyzing Business Scenario

Overview

Planners of innovative business projects at the first instance should analyze the business scenario around the market and evaluate its suitability to the market players, including consumers. Often companies undergo serious limitations in making complete analysis of the market scenario from the perspective, existing demand and competition, available resources, technology, and lifecycle of the innovative products. This chapter argues that scenario planning is an essential tool for developing innovative business projects. Understanding market scenarios is a superior way of visualizing a business project in order to help managers see how the business environment offers better strategic choices in carrying out innovative projects. Illustrating the experiences of various multinational companies, this chapter maps scenario for exploring innovative business projects in business-to-consumers and business-to-business sectors and offers ways to define the need for innovative differentiation. It is argued in the chapter that analyzing the sociopolitical determinants, and critically examining the micro- and macroeconomic factors would help the managers to develop competitive business projects within the existing business environment in a given marketplace. Doing this will bring organizational learning, enhance executive competencies, broaden project management perspectives, and help everyone involved in the innovative business projects to plan and implement projects in the complex and nonlinear business environment. The attributes of various decision drivers in reference to changing organizational cultures have also been discussed in this chapter.

Analyzing Business Environment

Business scenarios in the geodemographic segments across the markets are changing frequently over the years as the technology is rapidly growing.

The consumer preferences in food and beverages, electronics, home décor, over-the-counter pharmaceutical products, automobile, and office equipment have shown dynamic changes since the mid-20th century as companies are engaged continuously toward introducing innovative products to mark competitive advantage in the marketplace. Business scenarios in the business-to-business markets have also shown much advancement by automation of various operations within the company as well as within the network of market players engaged in operations. The growing trend of information technology (IT) has set many uphill challenges for the companies to adapt the automation process, which has driven several start-up companies to introduce innovative concepts through software applications in order to support the automation process. The global business scenario has been altered significantly by the Chinese companies that brought out innovative products in support of industrial automation process by encouraging small start-up enterprises (SUEs) and reached to a larger marketplace across the destinations. These companies are opening up a new front in the global competition based on reengineering the manufacturing and processes by improving the research and development, and innovation processes to introduce differentiation in the business performance at low prices. The innovative business projects in the emerging markets comprising Brazil, India, China, Russia, and South Africa initiated by both SUEs and large companies are carried out at economies of scale, when the marketing testing of innovative products and services are successful. As innovative business projects are largely managed at economies of scale, they turn to be cost-effective, low price, and sustainable for long run.

The emphasis on co-creation of innovation and managing innovation business projects partnering with the local companies is gradually generating technological breakthroughs, allowing emerging companies to reduce the time to bring innovative products and services to the market. The recent trend of carrying out innovation in the business-to-consumer as well as business-to-business segments by companies exhibits different ways of deploying cost and volume advantages in global competition by outsourcing innovation, partnering with SUEs, encouraging open innovation, and driving public–private partnerships. For example, companies from emerging markets like large manufacturers, such as Lenovo Group Ltd. (China), Godrej Consumer Products (India), and Internet players, such as Tencent Inc. (China), are pioneering new ways of industrializing innovation. These companies are engaged in simultaneous engineering by leveraging quick launch, test, and improve cycles combining vertical hierarchy for effective control of manufacturing systems with horizontal flexibility, allowing autonomy among the innovation teams to steer the new insights and experiments within peer groups. Lenovo acquired IBM's personal computer business in 2005 with its new product development cycle systems spanning 12 to 18 months. In view of growing competition in the laptop and desktop consumer segment, Lenovo geared-up innovation in this segment and has managed to reduce the product introduction cycle to nearly half of its predetermined span. In order to match the innovation and market dynamics, companies should grow as learning organization open to new ideas for driving differentiation, and accelerate continuous innovation across a wide range of industries reaching economies of scale at relatively low costs and acceptable quality that ensure value for money to the consumers. Innovative business projects catering to the emerging market demand and consumer needs are often risky and might not ensure breakthroughs in the market. However, successful implementation of innovative business projects have the potential to powerfully disrupt the profit models of competitors and make space in the market for the innovation to grow over the period. In order to gain manage the innovative business projects efficiently, companies should reengineer their internal innovation processes based on the principles of vertical and horizontal management approaches focusing on time-bound projects involving local partners or workforce (Williamson and Yin 2014).

Adequate capital resource is one of the major indicators for carrying out the innovative business projects successfully in the company. Innovative business projects fail because often companies face the budgetary and time constraints in managing such projects. The cost and time overruns in managing innovative business projects are common. Hence, companies should invest in data management systems, team-training programs, project-management software packages, and adapting best practices to support innovation. Whether a production process or a new-product-development project, the theory of constraints explains that managers of such projects should focus on the vital gaps in the project flow instead of working intensively on the stage-gate process of the projects, so that budget and time frame can be managed besides ensuring the quality of output (Elton and Roe 1998).

Continuous growth in innovation and technologies is the principal stimulant for the companies to gain competitive differentiation and leadership in the global markets, and high brand equity to drive consumers toward new buying preferences and explore new market segments. However, it is often hard for consumers to adopt innovations, gain confidence in deriving values appropriately, and derive competitive advantages from the innovative offerings over the existing and predetermined products and services. The consumer perceptions on the innovative products and technologies are largely influenced by the social and informal networks. Such interconnections among consumers and companies are so strong that often a new product's adoption by one player depends on its systematic adoption by other players. Traditionally, companies launch innovative products by targeting unique customer segments or developing compelling value propositions. However, companies engaged in continuous innovations orchestrate a change of behavior among consumers across the market segments in order to expand their market outreach. Companies engaged in innovation and competitive gains in the marketplace should explore new market segments, develop and implement strategies that maximize the chances of getting the competitive advantage, complement power players, and position the innovation as an enhancement to products or services. The innovation and technology companies tend to offer coordinated switching incentives to the players (social media, retailer, and salespeople) who add to the innovation's benefits, the players that act as channels to adopters and early adopters to ensure the value of the products and services (Chakravorti 2004). The elements of a business scenario in a destination market are woven around various macroeconomic factors comprising political, social, economic, technological, and legal factors beside the microeconomic factors within the company and market, as exhibited in Figure 2.1.

A business scenario in a destination country, region, or market is built around the macro- and microeconomic factors exhibited in Figure 2.1 that need to be explored by the companies to identify right innovation project and carry it successfully within the existing environment. The macroeconomic factors that affect the innovation management activities

- Political environment
- Investments, incentives, and monetary policies
- Social media, consumer networks
- Communication grid and media policies
- Technology governance
- Legal framework, patents, and IPR laws
- Consumption pattern
- Public economics, infrastructure, and public participation

- Organizational capabilities
- Managerial competencies
- Marketing-mix (11 Ps)
- Geo-demographic segments
- Market competition
- Returns on investment (Innovation)
- Commercialization and risk management
- Incremental innovation
- Strategic alliances on innovation

Macro-economic factors

Windows to innovation management projects

Micro-economic factors

Understanding business scenarios for innovation business projects

Regional attributes
- Developed economies
- Emerging markets
- Transition markets
- Globalization
- Local enterprises

Corporate ambience
- Size of the organization
- Business philosophy
- Corporate reputation
- Organizational culture

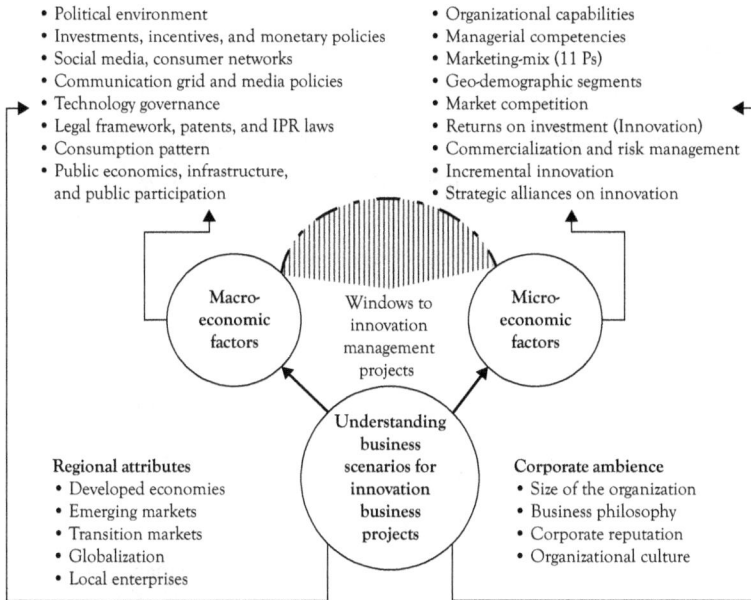

Figure 2.1 The environment of business innovation projects

in a company include political support toward innovations in reference to specific sectors, such as energy, public health, IT, low-cost construction, and other areas of public interest. The focus of the government toward investments, incentives, and monetary policies to support innovation and improve consumption culture also affects the companies toward undertaking innovative business projects and plan investment and returns accordingly. Consumers' engagement in social media to share new ideas across networks drive consumer innovation and technology governance significantly in the society. The macroeconomic factors differ across the developing economies, emerging markets, and local enterprises, but they have become a part of globalization, and influence the innovations in consumer markets. The microeconomic factors are largely confined within the business organization in reference to capabilities and competencies, and marketing-mix strategies of 11 Ps comprising product, price, place, promotion, packaging, pace (time), people (front liners), performance (brand line), psychodynamics (informal communication network), posture (corporate reputation), and proliferation (product extensions). Companies explore innovative business projects that are responsive to the market competition and fit into the consumer demand of specific geodemographic segments in order to avoid the risk and drive easy commercialization. The microeconomic factors of the innovation carrying companies also support the decision-making process of the companies toward developing strategic alliances with the SUEs and other companies anchoring innovative business projects, and carry incremental innovations over the previous generation of innovations. The microeconomic factors are also related to the size of the organization, business philosophy, and organization culture in carrying out innovation in the competitive marketplace.

Exploring Innovative Business Projects

Innovation is a continuous process and it helps organizations grow. Growth is often measured in terms of business performance, turnover, and profit, which occurs by bringing the competitive differentiation in the marketplace generating knowledge, consumer experience, quality or products, values, and marketing efficiency. Innovation is the process of making changes to something established by introducing something new. As such, it can be radical or incremental that can be applied to products, processes, or services, and in any organization. Innovation can be explored at all levels in an organization as well as in markets by generating consumer involvement in the new product or services development projects. In view of the fast growing market competition, more and more companies are recognizing innovation as the business opportunity created by a focus on sustainability. Such shift in thinking in many companies and industries, where learning-organization principles are being applied to create sustainable business models, has evidenced a change in organizational culture and improvement in the core competencies. Simultaneously, they become inspirational, energetic places to work, where even relationships with customers and suppliers improve. However, a more integrated view will enable companies to innovate for long-term profitability and sustainability. There are three core competencies that learning organizations must master to profit from sustainability, including encouraging systemic thinking, convene strategic market players and customers toward changing conventional thinking, and take the lead in reshaping the economic, political, and societal forces that baffle change (Senge and Carstedt 2001).

Often companies select innovative business projects in terms of its potential for commercialization and gaining high market share in the competitive marketplace. Such strategic thinking helps companies in carrying out innovations and business projects beyond commoditization, and fend off disruptive competitive threats to pave a path to enter new markets successfully. Innovative business projects lead toward transformational growth by determining news of engagement with customers and market players. Companies develop innovation projects with unique concepts with the goal to gain higher profit, brand image, and customer value to customers. Companies can successfully explore innovative business projects in the following manner by:

- Identifying the right innovative growth opportunities that could serve the latent demand in the market (where consumers are in need of the product but products are not available), tapping into a hidden or new customer needs with a completely new business model that builds the competitive advantage.
- Co-creating innovation projects by engaging customers and designing new business models to achieve desired project outcome efficiently and profitably.
- Successfully entering in global and local markets, penetrating the market competition to serve the latent needs of consumers by implementing the innovative business projects successfully.
- Creating new systems to support innovative business projects, and set new rules and metrics that enable companies to innovations successfully.

Innovative business projects are fundamentally rethinking of business around consumer needs by realigning corporate resources, processes, and profit formula with this new value propositions. The fundamental elements of a business project, which companies need to understand and manage during the project include variety of factors as discussed as follows:

- Definition of the project
- Characteristics of projects
- The Project Manager
- Attributes of project management
- Project Lifecycles
- The project environment
- Project selection
- Project planning
- Project finance
- Risk management
- Execution of project

Innovative business projects need not be picked up by the companies driven by emotions and impulse. They should be evaluated at the foreground in reference to the management capabilities as well as their potential for commercialization. Innovation projects often fail as they have a kick-start with loosely or sometimes ambiguously defined objectives, and project managers realize in the midstream of project process that it is going astray. Most SUEs tend to define innovation projects as experimental and exploratory projects and seldom follow loose linear guidelines, and suffer serious setbacks over the project stages. As innovation projects generally need to be sold to project sponsors and funding committees, project teams should be more involved and responsible while carrying out the projects. Innovative business projects are largely laid on multitask and multidecision, a process that is susceptible to risks and uncertainties between the project stages unless a well-developed set of criteria for the project has been developed in advance. Projects carrying out innovations should be time-bound to reduce the risk of commercialization and adaptation among consumers. However, sometime they are dragged on and on with endless tweaks and companies struggle to make adjustments to finish the project and launch the innovation in the market. The consumer involvement in the innovative business projects helps the companies launch innovations and its adoption faster. Hence, the current trend of identifying innovation projects for the companies are largely driven by the stimulating consumer involvement through various approaches of crowdsourcing. For example, Fiat Brazil developed a collaborative platform that combines crowdsourcing, open innovation, and creative commons in order to develop a model concept car called Fiat Mio. In the process of carrying out the innovative automobile project, the Fiat Mio team managed interactions over several months with 17,000 participants, from 160 different nationalities, and analyzed more than 11,000 ideas for developing appropriate innovation concept, its testing, and developing the prototype. The consumer belongingness to the innovation was evidenced by the company when Fiat Mio was launched in December 2010 at the Sao Paulo Auto Show as several people showed up to claim the prototype as their own. Submissions on the crowdsourcing platform allowed participants to communicate the idea of wheels that rotate 90° to make easier parallel parking and use of cameras instead of rearview mirrors and intervehicle communication to avoid collision. The Fiat Mio is a prime example of what can be accomplished with intelligent crowdsourcing of the new product development activities of a company. Such experiment has evidenced that instead of relying solely on internal abilities, connecting to a large community of engineers, startups, and other partners to circumvent the restrictions of limited resources and knowledge, and think outside-the-box could make the innovative business projects perform successfully (Saldanha and Pozzebon 2015). The process of exploring innovative business projects is exhibited in Figure 2.2.

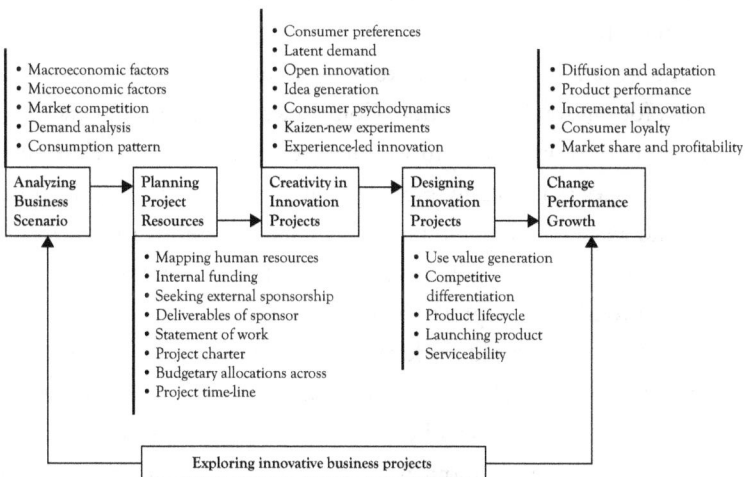

Figure 2.2 Process of exploring innovative business projects

Ideally, exploring innovative business projects is neither emotional nor a peer influence exercise for the companies. Most companies follow a predetermined path to explore the potential innovation to be carried out through standard project management process as exhibited in Figure 2.2. There are five stages that help the companies explore the innovation which that the market potential. In order to choose a product or services innovation, companies should analyze the macro- and microeconomic factors, market demand, and consumption patterns. Upon identifying the innovation to be carried out, the companies also need to identify internal capability and competence in managing innovation process, funding and sponsorship, develop statement of work (SOW), and project charter. The creativity in innovation projects should be based on analyzing consumer preferences, scope of open innovation, and carrying out "experience innovation" involving consumer and stakeholders of the company. Customer-centric companies develop innovation project designs that can generate high consumer use value, competitive differentiation, long and sustainable product lifecycle, and charter of serviceability of innovative products. While exploring the innovations to create competitive differentiation, most companies face the challenge of diffusion of knowledge about the innovation, and inducing adaptability among consumers. It is necessary for the companies also to identify the scope of incremental innovation to carry out further improvements on the innovation in order to develop consumer loyalty, and augment market share and profit contribution of the innovation.

The innovation strategy defines the role of innovation and sets the direction for innovation execution. Companies should explore innovative business opportunities close to the market demand and develop innovation strategies that actually provide them leverage to launch the innovation and make a profitable business in the competitive marketplace. Incremental innovations are carried out by the consumer-centric companies as a routine to improve the business performance of the existing products. Companies build market value through continuous innovation, which is derived by exploring new and incremental innovation business projects, connecting the dots between many singular ideas and crowdsourced into one big platform innovation, and fully scaling it to maximize the potential benefits. The good innovative business projects should exhibit the potential to generate "me too" feeling upon its commercialization. Research proves that companies that successfully apply a structured process to innovation project management reduce risk in the business process and increase the results of innovation. The criteria associated with a strong innovation should be to develop influencing, ambitious, high perceived use value, and adaptive innovations in the marketplace with unique adaptable propositions. The specific characteristics of innovative business projects should include the following attributes:

- Projects have an established objective
- Projects have a well-defined life span
- Projects require staff participation from across the organization
- Projects have a defined schedule and budgets
- Projects have limited resources
- Projects have multiple, often competing stakeholders

Innovative business projects exhibit change, cross-functionality, uniqueness, and uncertainty as major attributes. A project carrying out innovative business ideas engages people from different seniority and business departments, who work together during the period of the project. For instance, to develop sales software, people from marketing and sales departments should work closely with the IT department. Companies should understand that each innovative business project should be unique, cost-effective, time-bound, and able to generate high customer value. Projects might be divided into the different task segments and should be treated as unique. However, carrying out projects with unique propositions drives uncertainty. An innovative business project is a one-time, once-off activity, never to be repeated exactly the same way again. Hence, the projects are set within specific timeframe. Once the goal is achieved, the organization created for it is disbanded or sometimes it is reconstituted to begin working on a new project. Innovative business projects should be developed on a single definable purpose, process, and outcome. This is usually specified in terms of cost, schedule, and performance requirements. Projects always cut across the regular organizational lines and structures within a firm, because they need to draw the skills and the talents of multiple professions and departments within the firm and sometimes even from other organizations. The complexity of advanced technology often leads to additional project difficulties by creating task interdependencies that may introduce new and unique problems.

Defining and Managing Projects

Managing innovative business projects is a set of functions related to the application of knowledge, process and implementation skills, and project tools and techniques to perform activities to meet the project requirements (Hamel and Tennant 2015). It is necessary for the company to define the projects clearly to carry them out without any problem in moving the tasks through the project pathway and having the ease of decision making at each stage-gate of the project charter. Companies need to consider the following factors while defining the innovative business projects aimed at commercialization in the completive marketplace across geodemographic segments:

- Identifying all the requirements, including consumer needs, competition, organizational capability and competence, budgetary requirements, risk management, and compatibility of project with the existing macro- and microeconomic factors.
- Establishing clear and achievable objectives.
- Balancing the competing demands for quality, scope, time, and costs.
- Adapting to the specifications, plans, and expectations of the various stakeholders.

A study on development projects at Chaparral Steel, Digital Equipment, Eastman Kodak, Ford Motor, and Hewlett-Packard reveal that the innovative business projects are small-scale version of an organization and should be carried out parallel to the organizational dynamics. These project could generate powerful, distinctive capabilities upon designing and implementing the project processes meticulously. The most successful projects demonstrate core capabilities, guiding visions, organization and leadership, ownership and commitment, prototypes, and integration

(Bowen et al. 1994). In order to remain innovative, companies thrive to develop new products and processes with an objective to implement them rapidly and gain consumer attention. Innovation and its ability to create competitive advantage depend on how dynamic a company is on staying vigilant on the innovative concepts of SUEs, analyzing market information, and developing marketable innovations. Each innovation has different value proposition for the consumers over different spatial and temporal situations. Companies learn innovative ideas largely from crowdsourcing. *Open Innovation* is one of the central concepts for gaining competitive advantage in the marketplace. Open Innovation implies that innovation processes increasingly require collaboration with several stakeholders, users, suppliers, and experts.

3M Company explored an innovative business project, which has high market potential in the Taiwanese market. The project team of the company exploited the local market needs for 3M Hydrocolloid Dressing, a technology that had existed in the company for many years, but no practical applications were found for commercialization. The local project team suggested applying the material for acne treatment of young consumers. The product would be known as Acne Dressing. As there was no standardized solution for acne treatment in Taiwan, the company decided to develop Acne Dressing as a brand-new product in the local market. However, the biggest challenge for the company was to make the innovation adaptable to the consumers and change local consumer behaviors on new acne-treatment products. Finally, 3M Company launched the Acne Dressing Patches in the Taiwanese market in 2011 with Nexcare brand as the first product application of the company from Hydrocolloid Dressing technology (Williams and Emily 2014).

Companies should define innovative project work with clear SOW as a reference for guiding the innovation projects clearly within the teams. An SOW is a formal document that captures and defines the work activities, deliverables, and timeline a vendor must execute in performance of specified work for a client. The SOW usually includes detailed requirements and pricing, with standard regulatory and governance terms and conditions. It, thus, overlaps in concept with a contract and indeed SOWs are often legally equivalent to contracts. The SOW can be also constituted with a participatory approach involving all members of the innovation team using the Goal Oriented Project Planning (GOPP) approach. In this approach, all members of the innovation team are asked to share their one best response on the project goal, sponsor, project process, approach toward tasks, timeline, deliverables, and potential problems in carrying the project. SOW can be developed by categorizing response on each element of GOPP and later forming an appropriate statement that could serve as the guiding tool for carrying out the innovative business projects. SOW should also delineate the scope of the project, external bids for generating resources in case the innovative business project to be sponsored externally, and description of products and services sponsored by the funding company or organization. The project team should develop a project charter upon forming the SOW, which is a statement of the scope, objectives, and participants in a project and is a critical document to ensure that everyone involved in the project is aware of its purpose and objectives. The project charter is usually a short document that refers to more documents related to the project and also include the "Terms of Reference" of project. The purpose of the project charter is to document the following perspectives in detail:

- Reasons for undertaking the project
- Objectives and constraints of the project
- Directions concerning the solution
- Identities of the main stakeholders
- In-scope and out-of-scope items
- High-level risk management plan
- Communication plan
- Target project benefits
- High-level budget and spending authority

Organizational culture largely determines the ways of achieving outcomes of innovative business projects in reference to the local and global markets. The cultural influence in an organization includes the employee protocol that talks about problems and solutions, workspaces, and temporal rhythms of work. Social interactions on innovation need to interfere with the local innovation project teams, market players, and consumers to explore the marketability of the innovation product and its possible lifecycle to determine the process of incremental innovation and prospects of the next generation of innovation. The impact of innovation work must be redefined to include more than reporting on the data that demonstrates outcomes. Impact includes the entire process of innovating business project management and actions that leads the innovation adaptation among the consumers. The best practices for managing the innovative business projects are woven around the following factors:

- Customer need and benefit
- Alignment with the market, product, and technology strategy
- Market and customer attractiveness
- Financial return on investment (ROI)
- R&D, manufacturing, and supply chain feasibility
- Competitiveness
- Sales and distribution factors

The need for innovation and attributes of the innovative products needs to be methodically defined, so that upon completion of the innovation process, it could deliver consistent and profitable breakthroughs. The innovation breakthroughs could be attained by skills, tools, metrics, processes, platforms, incentives, managerial roles, and values. Companies can achieve success in launching the innovations by managing the innovation projects considering various challenges within the company. Innovative business projects are taken up by the companies not only to achieve market leadership through competitive differentiation, but also to overcome the conventional business practices existing within the company over a long period. As the markets tend to grow manifold and stay dynamic, in any company, managerial and operational models lean to converge with the current practices over time. The innovation ideas emerge effectively within the company, provided the managers stay attentive to the market development, and shifts in consumer preferences. In their quest to overturn industry rules, they learn how to distinguish the needed change in the business practice of the company against the ingrained beliefs. A business project for carrying out an innovation could be successful, provided the company is able to harness the latent demand among the target consumer segments and drive the innovation to meet the underappreciated trends. Innovators, SUEs, and companies pay attention to the changing consumer preferences and consumption pattern to explore the right opportunity for developing a new innovative product, following the standard project management process. To bring a successful innovation to the marketplace, companies need to take a long-term perspective than a myopic approach and develop an appropriate business model for launching and managing the innovation in the competitive marketplace. Defining and managing innovative business projects in a company involve three different scenarios comprising internal fit, external fit, and phases of innovation project, as illustrated in Figure 2.3.

The innovation projects move through the three conventional phases comprising preproject phase, implementation phase, and postproject phase. Companies explore business opportunities, develop business plans, and obtain seed funding in the preproject phase. As the project moves further to the implementation phase, the innovation project team engages in defining innovation, developing design, developing project charter, and building prototype and its testing. In the postimplementation

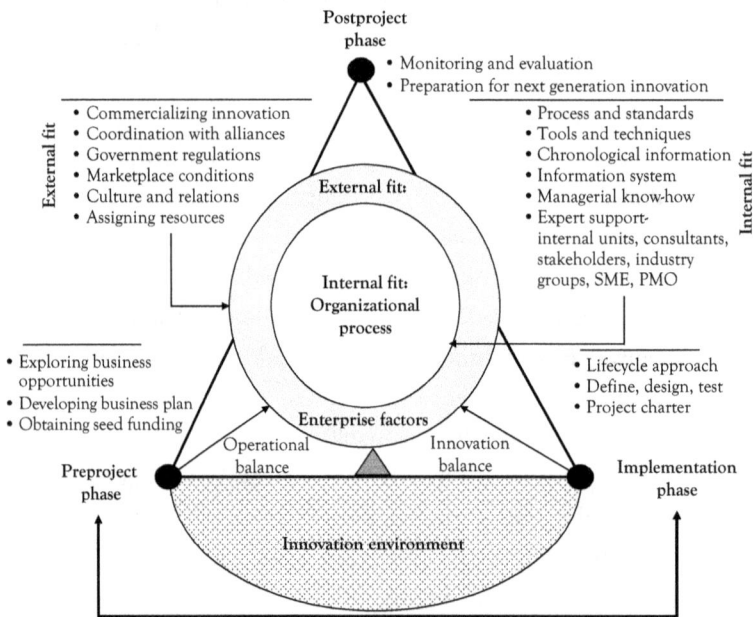

Figure 2.3 *Innovation projects phases and fit within the business environment*

phase of the innovative project, companies are engaged in monitoring, evaluation, and preparing for the next generation of innovation. The external fit of innovation projects is woven around the enterprise factor comprising tasks for commercialization of innovation, coordination, and alliances with external companies and SUEs, understanding marketplace conditions, and assigning resources to carry innovations with the social and government norms. Besides, the internal fit for innovative business projects involves developing process and standards for carrying out innovations in a company by determining appropriate tools and techniques, building managerial know-how, and offering expert supports within the organizations.

Zara, a successful fast-fashion manufacturer and retailer from Spain is quoted in the business lessons for its uncommon business process and building its popular flagship through setting a sustainable strategic vision. The company produces fashion apparel with marginal investment on advertising, overspends on positioning their fashion innovations in the high-end stores, and carries substantially less inventory and sets the prices for its products less than its competitors. The investors of the company initially disagreed with this strategy of the company to market fashion and innovative design apparel. However, the company has proven its strategy of low-cost sensitization of innovative design garments in the high- and low-end markets by establishing as a brand leader in the industry and in emerging markets with its strategy for success. New competitors and growing business disruptions in market threaten alternate innovations that might beat the original innovation of company by successfully copying key components of the successful innovations of the company (Doiron 2015). Emerging companies need to define the innovative business projects, considering the following fundamental characteristics of the project:

- Process
  - Grouping, inputs, and outputs
  - Initiating, planning, executing, and closing
- Develop a project charter
- Identify stakeholders
- Develop work breakdown structure

A successful innovation process should undergo proper grouping of task and plan for continuous flow of inputs and outputs at various stages of managing the innovative business projects. It requires timely initiation of the project, planning and execution of tasks, and proper closing the project in order to deliver the innovative product, which has the best fit to the marketplace. Developing a comprehensive project charter as a guiding tool for carrying out the innovation and identifying stakeholder of the innovative projects leading to commercialize are considered to be the project pillars. Innovation projects should also have a clear work breakdown structure (WBS) based on the project tasks, time, and deliverables that should be divided across various stages and review gates of the project plan. Innovation often gets thwarted if selected on the self-reference basis, which is largely derived on the emotions of the top management or the impulsive competitive pressure of the market. Such projects tend to fail as they are not developed around customer needs, predetermined core competencies, and strategic goals of the company. Start-up enterprises and amateur innovators review their capability and competence, and the market around them as a portfolio of skills and assets that can be recombined continuously in developing new products and businesses.

Most customers have resistance toward adapting to the new products, which hinders the performance and growth of new and innovative products in the marketplace. Thus, the companies launching new products should develop comprehensive innovation diffusion plan including do-it-yourself product demonstration, product advertisements, and communication on the social media, in order to develop product attractiveness as well as confidence in consumer adaptation to the new products. To manage innovation in a systematic way, it is important for the companies to define innovation and its marketing prospects that would give the company a real feel about the innovation and calculate its pay-offs over the period. Developing "applied innovation" is harder than the "concept innovation" products as a product might stay beyond the popular conventions of consumerism and lack in innovativeness that stimulates the consumers. Cosmetic innovation, such as if a company puts ketchup in a new squeeze bottle, is neither a new nor incremental innovation. However, some marketing strategies that push innovation with value additions could make the innovative products move in the market along with the competitive products. For example, when Comcast, an Internet and media channel providing company in the United States, rolls out a new "triple play" pricing scheme, it not only drives the IT breakthrough, but also promotes consumerism toward the product. An incremental innovation may be described in reference to a consumer goods company, which launches a washing machine that dispenses just the right amount of detergent. This innovation may stay popular as a game-changer in the competitive marketplace. For a product to be innovative in many consumer products companies, it must be unique and compelling to the consumer, create a competitive advantage, have potential to induce incremental innovations, and provide consumers with more value than the available products in the market. The innovation performance can be measured using the following elements of the innovation dashboard:

- **Inputs**: The vital inputs for carrying out innovations include capital, funding investors, raw material, engineering support, employee time devoted to innovation, and timeline from initiation to launch of innovation along with the number of ideas that are generated internally and outside the organization from customers, suppliers, and retailers.

- **Pipeline concepts**: Companies get abundant new ideas through crowdsourcing, and it is often a major task to filter the quality ideas to enter the pipeline after initial screening. The filtered ideas or opportunities for innovation are carried forward through a business project, wherein their transition from concept to prototype to commercialization takes longer within the innovation pipeline.

- **Outputs**: From the point of view of commercialization, the outreach of number of innovations in a given market over the determined timeframe and the percentage of revenue derived from new products and services constitute the innovation output.

- **Leadership**: Innovations are generally successful, provided such business projects are backed by the strong leadership. Companies prescribe higher percentage of executive time to be devoted toward mentoring and managing innovation projects and generate proinnovation culture in the organization.

- **Competence**: Innovation-oriented companies believe that the higher the percentage of employees trained as business innovators, the better the quality of innovation. Accordingly, companies are recruiting qualified innovation *black belts* with expertise on lean manufacturing not only to supervise the innovation projects, but also to serve as change agents in diffusion and adaptation of innovation among consumers.
- **Ambience**: Innovation can be successfully managed if the organizational culture and infrastructure (microenvironment) and the sociobusiness scenario (macroenvironment) are favorable to the innovation process. If the infrastructure for innovation is inadequate, it leads to premature termination of innovation projects, and the investments made toward the innovation projects are often runs as sunk cost.
- **Project balance**: The efficiency of innovation projects is governed by the cost and time ratio that determine the ratio of input and output of an innovation. The mix of different types of innovation, such as product, service, pricing, distribution, operations, and so on, lead to different risk categories, including incremental improvements and cost and time overrun.

As the competition in the global marketplace is increasing, more and more companies are recognizing that their experience with consumers across the geodemographic segments about competitive products are value additions to develop new capabilities within the organization for carrying out innovations. However, managing a global innovation project in the same conventional style of single-location projects would be a very difficult proposition for the companies in reference to size, resources, and contingencies. Single-location projects draw on tacit knowledge and shared experience, unlike the global projects lack. The management challenge among the companies is, therefore, to replicate the positive developing "experience innovation" across the geo-demographic segments while harnessing the opportunities of innovation dispersion (Wilson and Doz 2012).

The recent trend among large companies toward exploring new innovation insights is leaning toward analyzing the innovation tactics and management practices with the local enterprises in emerging markets. Digging deep into the enterprises at the bottom-of-the-pyramid, the multinationals are starting to catch on to the logic of reverse innovation, in which the products are designed first for consumers in low-income geodemographic segments and then adapted into disruptive offerings for developed markets. However, only few companies have managed to do it successfully until recently. It has been observed in various studies that the main problem in carrying out the reverse innovation is the mindset of innovators and sponsoring companies. One of the major challenges in the reverse innovation is matching segments to the existing products, lowering price by removing features, mismatch of technical requirements, convincing stakeholders, and agreeing to developing low-cost innovation products for low-income markets could have global appeal (Govindarajan and Winter 2015).

Understanding Consumers for Innovation Adaptation

Launching innovations in a predetermined marketplace is easier for a company than pushing the innovation among the consumer segments for adaptation, as this is a cognitive process unlike a systematic project management path. The cognitive response on any new product is a complex phenomenon independent of several business-related factors visualized by the companies. Consumers largely depend on crowd cognition process to accept a new product, in which they keep updating their knowledge through social media, consumer blogs, friends and family, and business newspapers and magazines. In such cognition process, consumers set or update beliefs, expectation, and establish relation with their previous experience. If the product is relatively new and of high technology, consumers tend to collect information on the product extensively and also keep alternate brands on their shopping cart. There is a relatively smaller consumer segment, which develops self-reference criterion and takes the decision on adapting the new innovative product with confidence instead of seeking second opinion.

Most companies struggle to educate consumers toward adapting new innovative products for a change, with an impulse tag such as Smart consumer electronics or Diet consumer products. However, such tags also raise questions among consumers as the communications associated with tags are not clear to drive the right perceptions among the consumers. Such situations are more complex for consumers, and companies bring the new products that have identical attributes into the gamut of buying behavior. For example, a native purified water-bottling company Bonafont in Mexico, initially launched the purified water in peach color bottles to position it through the psychographic segmentation for women consumers. Later as the product reached the growth stage, the company developed a sense of diet product among the consumers through a television commercial that visualized a petite women walking into the elevator along with others preboarded trigged the elevator to go up as against a situation earlier when the elevator indicated overload. Such stimuli help the new products, whether identical or similar in attributes, to inculcate positive perception toward adapting them against those existing in the market. The adaptation of consumers to new innovations and technologies is largely based on the efficiency of the companies in diffusing the innovation among consumer before the launch of innovation or simultaneously during the launch. Figure 2.4 exhibited the reasons associated with the low adaptation among consumers to the innovative products and services.

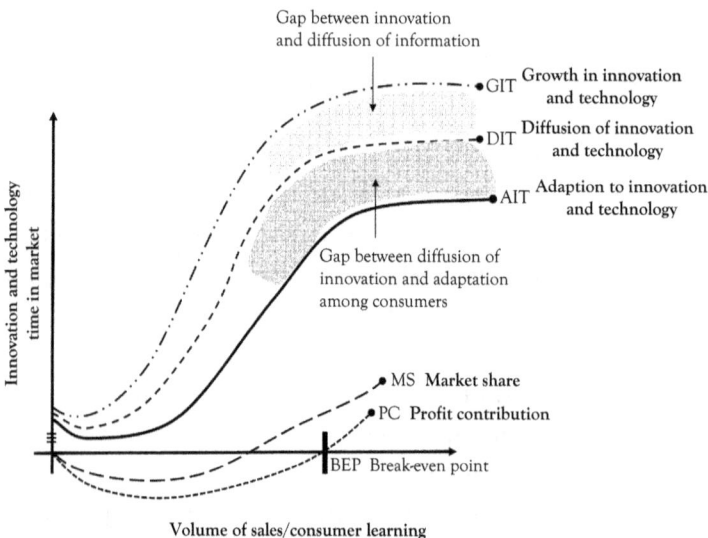

Figure 2.4 Diffusion and adaptation of innovation and related consequences

It has been evidenced since the mid-20th century that the innovation and technology (GIT) is growing at a faster pace than the companies are able to diffuse information on innovation and technology (DIT) among consumers in the marketplace as illustrated in Figure 2.4. As the time management for DIT < GIT, companies have prolonged break-even point (BEP) of innovative products they launch in the market due to initial low market share for, and slow growth of sales of, new technology-led innovative products. Hence, companies should develop suitable consumer education and demonstration policies for innovative products before or during the early launch period to disseminate competitive advantages with unique selling proposition. Innovation companies partner with other enterprises to develop innovation diffusion and consumer communication, including social media communication, advertising, and interactive learning projects like do-it-yourself activities, in-store demonstrations, one-on-one communication with consumers, and telemarketing.

The company-consumer interlocking through effecting diffusion strategies of innovative products works efficiently through the interpersonal communication on social networks and direct marketing approaches. Firms can use to build relationships with co-creative business partners that are more suited to explore new opportunities to unveil innovations among consumers and face emerging threats in new competitive environments to drive the consumption of innovative products sustainable. However, companies should identify the key barriers that prevent networks for discontinuous innovation and presents specific strategies that can stimulate the adaptation process for new products. In order to build synergy among the growth of innovation and technology approaches, and diffusion of innovation strategies, companies may face various challenges, including finding the right partners to engage with, forming relationships with consumers, and then building high-performing innovation dissemination networks (Birkinshaw, Bessant, and Delbridge 2007).

Marketing innovative products and technology solutions along with a bundle of services is a priority in today's increasingly competitive markets. Companies, however, are not always structured and capable of making such integration in their products and services offerings in the market to gain competitive advantage. Thus, most companies prefer to engage in price competition rather than delivering customer value through integrated products and services. Knowledge and competencies of the company are intangible factors to harness consumer value. Multinational companies like GE Healthcare, Best Buy, and AT&T, have restructured themselves around customer need to deliver customer-focused solutions by information sharing, division of labor, and value-based decision making. Customer-centric companies, such as Cisco Systems, have developed customer satisfaction matrix and laid policies that support incentives in rewarding customer-focused cooperation. Delivering customer-focused solutions requires a mix of employees in an organization to be generalists, instead of specialists. The customer-focused solutions team requires experience with more than one product or service, a deep knowledge of customer needs, and the ability to traverse internal boundaries. By combining the aforementioned attributes companies, we can create cost-effective high-value solutions and stand out in a competitive market (Gulati 2007).

The benefits of customer-centric management include increasing efficiency and effectiveness in maintaining current customers rather than prospecting new customers, and improved competitive advantage. The consumer benefits through consumer learning in such situations can be stored, processed, and retrieved to use in subsequent situations. This leads to an ability to manage future decisions based on simplifying problem-solving situations and reducing risk (Sharma and Seth 1997). Market orientation strategy and customer-centric marketing approaches together have a significant impact on the performance of new products and technologies of the company. Managers should integrate the market orientation and customer services strategies to enhance the customer value. One of the challenges for the dealer firms is to incorporate preferences of the customer into overall performance and services in order to maximize the customer value. An augmented and sustainable customer value builds loyalty toward the product and the brand.

Traditional approaches to innovation strategy of both SUEs and large companies assume that the world is relatively stable and predictable. But globalization, new technologies, and greater transparency have combined to overturn the business environment. Such shift in the business environment has generated more risk and vulnerability among companies in engaging with new innovative projects. Hence, managers are increasingly finding the need to develop organizational capabilities to foster competitive advantage rapidly for encouraging adaptation to innovations among consumers. Instead of frequently innovating a new product that could overlap with the previous products of the company launched in the short span, they should explore prospective innovation partners who could take the responsibility of developing and implementing the consumer information strategies. Companies should also be good at learning how to co-create new things by earning the confidence of market players like business partners, distributors, retailers, and consumers. Companies that thrive to follow the integrate innovation strategies as discussed earlier can alter the consumer behavior quickly and manage the market demand. In order to achieve a sustainable market for innovative products, companies need to experiment rapidly and frequently not only with products and services, but also with business models, processes, and strategies. It is also necessary for the innovation-driven companies to acquire the skills to manage complex multistakeholder systems in an increasingly interconnected world of consumers (Reeves and Deimler 2011).

Customer needs should be appraised continuously by the managers, and appropriate changes should be proposed in a timely manner, which would help in improving market effectiveness, services efficiency, and dealer performance. It is commonly perceived by the marketing managers that a market-oriented campaign is expensive, but actually, it can lower operating costs and increase market share, yielding high sales. It is more profitable for a technology-marketing firm to establish long-term customer relationships than to adopt a short-term transaction-oriented approach. The customer-centric strategies in a firm should go beyond customer relationship and cater to cross-functional integration of processes, people, operations, and marketing capabilities, which is enabled through information, technology, and applications (Payne and Frow 2005).

Implementation of effective customer-centric strategies by the technology-marketing firms results in developing TIC effect among consumers. TIC effect is comprised with three cognitive factors, including trust, involvement, and commitment, thereby driving consumer behavior in a given marketplace. In a retail environment, trust may be understood as a concept that is often related to a customer's willingness to rely upon technology-marketing firm's services quality and customer relations. This concept represents quality in the sense that it helps to reduce uncertainty in complex consumer-retailer relationships (Bruhn 2003). Consumers' involvement with the technology-marketing firm, store brand, and promotions develop loyalty in the long run. When consumers feel satisfaction having their association with the retail brand, their sense of commitment and involvement is enhanced. Higher levels of involvement lead to greater levels of consumer loyalty and a lower need for scarce marketing resources. Hence, involvement does play a significant moderating role, and in most cases, the relationships with the technology-marketing firms and their store brands are stronger for consumers with higher involvement (Baker, Cronin, and Hopkins 2009). Commitment as a concept is closely associated with the customer relationship strategy, where two parties lean toward loyalty and show stability to each other. A common opinion is that customer commitment only relates to a seller or a relationship with a seller. It is also observed that a high commitment level might be seen as an important emotional barrier in switching behavior (Hulten 2007). Customer relationships with retailers are dependent on specific cultural contexts, in which buyers and sellers interact, and the type of relationship developed over the period determines the strength of commitment.

Large innovation-led companies associating their innovation process with the SUEs serve customers through a broad array of interfaces, from retail sales customer relations team to website teams managing voice-response telephone systems to educate consumers on innovations as well as to resolve their problems. However, typical companies believe in investing on various consumer interface tools, but might not use any impressive interface collections due to weak interface system that requires upgrading skills of employees managing such interfaces. Most companies have the impression that smaller set of people and too many machines operating with insufficient coordination tend to raise complexity, costs, and customer dissatisfaction. Such corporate beliefs are turned wrong with the experience of automobile companies despite the plant and process automation, as the employees work with clear division of labor. In a world where companies compete not on what they sell, but on how they sell it, they could easily establish their innovation, brand, services, and customer relations despite the odds in market competition (Rayport and Jaworski 2004).

As consumer goods manufacturing companies and technology marketing channels tailor their value propositions to better address customer needs beyond product specifications and to better align their cost of sales and fulfillment relative to those needs, go-to-market (GTM) strategy plays a central role. To compensate for less-frequent product launches and a focus on integrated solutions rather than specific products, Microsoft now organizes its marketing efforts around annual GTM campaigns. GTM strategies focus Microsoft and its partners on short-term strategic challenges and provide consistent marketing approaches for most of its business products. GTM strategies address the lack of new product releases on which to hang marketing campaigns by identifying a strategic issue facing Microsoft and constructing a framework for addressing it with broad-reach advertising, sales tools for partners and the Microsoft field sales force, and customer and partner incentives. There are as many as 11 determinants of the consumer behavior that influence in buying process. These factors include economic, relational, and personality-led factors that affect the consumer psychology in making buying decisions, getting associated with the product and developing loyalty toward the product, brand, or a retail store.

Customer satisfaction is perceived to be a key driver of long-term relationships between retailer and customers, especially when customers are well-acquainted with products and markets, and when industries are highly competitive. Technology-marketing efficiency is one of the principal factors, which influences customer satisfaction in a business-to-consumer and consumer-to-consumer context. This would help in building customer–retailer dyadic relationship. The key services indicators, which include effective communication, cross-functional teams, and supplier integration, are followed to develop long-term relationships. Customer satisfaction has long been considered a milestone in the path toward profitability of technology marketing firms. It is widely acknowledged that satisfaction leads to higher market share and stable revenues, while relationship between customer satisfaction levels and quality of customer services influence acquisition of new customers (Rajagopal 2010). High-technology products sales are positively associated with the performance of retailers and distributors in terms of customer service quality, growth in sales, and increase in market share. Manufacturing and services elasticity are widely recognized as critical components in achieving competitive advantage in the marketplace and improving corporate reputation to augment customer value without escalating costs and time overrun.

The need for the competitively advantageous strategies may further be justified, as a large number of firms are increasingly productive in reference to the rapid diffusion of the technologies. The customers' bargaining power also works out to be an instrument to either broaden or narrow the differences between the competitors. The companies that use intermediaries are often encountered with the task of balancing the power of distribution and delivery of services. In consumer markets, the retail trade is forcing major concessions on the multinational brands. Such strategies hold the access to the retail network through a long chain of channels. Conventionally, the choice of appropriate scale in business and scope thereof were guided by the concepts of the bigger is better and umbrella control of activities. In the current era of globalization, the decentralization of activities and production sharing have become more effective tools in marketing. The profit center approach (PCA), control circles, and total quality management practices have endorsed the success of small integrated units operating in a well-defined market. In view to promote the PCA concepts and maintain the control circles, large companies are increasingly creating the autonomous, small, and entrepreneurial units to find responsive solutions to the customer problems in the well-defined market niches (Frederick 1989). Corporate structures are changing in order to accommodate the concept of PCA and control circles and are exploring for the long-term advantages by way of heavy investment to develop the core competencies.

The technological changes are the main impetus behind new market opportunities. The extent of such change may be explained from super technologies to the appropriate and intermediate technologies. The strategic choices have wide-ranging ripple effects through the organization that determine the key success factors and growth performance. Some companies would be making right strategic choices by improving the implementation process of competitive advantages. These companies are guided by the shared strategic vision and are driven by the responsive attitude toward the market requirements. They emphasize the continuous strive to satisfy the customers. A strategic vision in managing markets may be understood as the guiding theme that explains the nature of business and the future projections thereof. These projections or business intentions depend on the collective analysis of the environment that determines the need for the new developments or diversifications. The vision should be commissioned on a concrete understanding of the business and the ability to foresee the impact of market forces on the growth of business. The vision will motivate the organization for collaborative business planning and implementation. The powerful visions are also the statements of intent that create an obsession with winning throughout the organization (Day 1990).

Product strategies specify the market needs that may be served by different product offerings. The product strategies of the company are duly related to market strategies that eventually come to dominate both the overall strategy and the spirit of the company. Product strategies deal with matters such as the number and diversity of products, product innovations, product scope, and product design. In many companies, to achieve proper coordination among diverse business units, product strategy decisions are made by the top management. In some companies, the overall scope of product strategy is laid out at the corporate level, whereas the actual design is left to business units. Such alternative is more desirable than other arrangements because it is difficult for the top management to deal with the details of product strategy in a diverse company.

Each strategy is examined from the point of view of a business unit or profit center. The term positioning refers to placing a brand in that part of the market where it will receive a favorable reception compared to competing products. Because the market is heterogeneous, one brand cannot make an impact on the entire market. As a matter of strategy, therefore, a product should be matched with the consumer segment of the market in which it is most likely to succeed. The product should be positioned so that it stands apart from the competing brands. Positioning tells what the product stands for, what it is, and how customers should evaluate it. Positioning is achieved by using marketing mix variables, especially design and communication. Although differentiation through positioning is more visible in consumer goods, it is equally true of industrial goods. With some products, positioning can be achieved on the basis of tangible differences (e.g., product features); with many others, intangibles are used to differentiate and position products.

Product choice among consumers will be difficult when products have marginal differentiation in reference to attributes, price, and use value as compared to the competing products available in the market. Hence, many manufacturing and technology-marketing firms provide default options to consumers in order to make their buying process easy. Well-designed defaults benefit both company and consumer, simplifying the buying-decision process of consumers, enhancing the level of satisfaction, reducing risk in purchases, and driving profitable purchases. On the contrary, misconceived options to choose products can leave money on the table, fuel consumer backlashes, put customers at risk, and trigger lawsuits costing companies dearly (Goldstein et al. 2008). As the competition among the companies manufacturing consumer goods and the number of routes to market are increasing, customers today are being forced with an overwhelming array of choices. Thus, companies should stop creating new brands and product extensions to alleviate customer frustration and consolidate product and service functions by following a four R approach, comprising replace, repackage, reposition, and replenish. In the race of acquiring and retaining strategies tested by the companies, customers are rapidly becoming smarter than the companies that pretend to serve them (Locke 2000). The desired position for a product may be determined using the following procedure:

- Analyze product attributes that are salient to customers.
- Examine the distribution of these attributes among different market segments.
- Determine the optimal position for the product with regard to each attribute, taking into consideration the positions occupied by the existing brands.
- Choose an overall position for the product (based on the overall match between product attributes and their distribution in the population and the positions of the existing brands).

Companies of consumer and industrial goods seek competitive distinction through product features—some visually or measurably identifiable, some cosmetically implied, and some rhetorically claimed by reference to real or suggested hidden attributes that promise results or values different from those of competitors' products. The offered product is differentiated, though the generic product is identical.

Macro- and Microeconomic Factors

The analysis of factors of production is an important consideration in international marketing to optimize the comparative advantages over natural resources, labor, capital, and entrepreneurship. Entrepreneurs, thus, play an important role in enabling the economy to adapt to the changing conditions and to new possibilities for material improvements, by creating new production organizations, and even to whole new industries. Because of its essential role in initiating the process of production, entrepreneurship is identified by some economists as a "fourth factor of production," alongside land, labor, and capital. It may, thus, be explained that higher the productivity of a factor of production, higher may be the income for the company. On the other hand, anything that rises above the expected levels of productivity within a society is responsible for increase in the overall prosperity of the society.

The price indicators in the international markets broadly include export and import price indexes, consumer prices, wholesale prices, and industrial producer prices. The export and import price indexes can be used to determine the impact of exchange rate movements on the prices of exports and imports. International price data have been useful for both multilateral and bilateral trade agreements, as often the countries utilize them to negotiate trade agreements for some of the important industrial and consumer products, such as construction material, plantation crop products like tea and coffee, cotton textiles, oil, airfreight services, and so on. A primary reason for measuring import prices is to track the impact they have on domestic inflation. The movement in import prices can often be an indicator of future inflation since some inputs to domestic production and consumption are imported. Export and import price indexes are essential for assessing the impact of international trade on the domestic economy. Some of their most important uses are analyzing developments in the trade balance, measuring domestic inflation, and deflating nominal values of exports and imports for estimating the volume of gross domestic product (GDP). The Producer Price Index (PPI) is a family of indexes that measures the average change over time in selling prices received by the domestic producers of goods and services. PPIs measure price change from the perspective of the seller. This contrasts with other measures, such as the Consumer Price Index (CPI) that measures price change from the purchaser's perspective. Sellers' and purchasers' prices may differ due to government subsidies, sales and excise taxes, and distribution costs. It is difficult for a marketer to access information about, and review all these indicators from, each country. However, at any given time, the choice of economic indicators may be identified to determine the entry strategies of a firm. These indicators may reflect on the marketer's domestic operations and the potential business in the host country.

Economic development is directly proportional to the educational and training facilities available in the country. Human resources are not only producers of goods and services, but also their consumers, they play a multifold role in economic development. Economic advancement is characterized by the following factors:

- Allocation of labor force to agriculture
- Energy available in large amounts at low cost per unit
- High level of GDP and income
- High levels of per capita consumption
- Relatively low rates of population growth
- Complex modern facilities for transportation, communication, and exchange
- Substantial amount of capital for investment
- Urbanization based on production as well as exchange
- Diversified manufacturing that accounts for an important share of the labor force
- Technology that includes ample media and methods for experiment

These factors may be utilized to examine economic standing of the host country, and an analysis of a large variety of information on these variables may help to categorize the countries on an economic development scale.

Besides, many historical, geographic, political, and cultural factors are intimately related to the economic well-being of a nation. Companies moving their production and business operations to the new destinations should meticulously review the macroeconomic conditions and analyze the correlations among the various macroeconomic indicators to take an appropriate decision.

A careful analysis of a microenvironment indicates whether a company can successfully enter a specific market. It can be stated that prosperity of a nation depends on the productivity with which it uses its human capital and natural resources. It is manifested in the way a nation's firms compete. Productivity, in turn, is a function of the interplay of many factors, including political, legal and macroeconomic context; the quality of the microeconomic business environment; and the sophistication of company operations and strategy. Together they determine the capacity of a nation to create internationally competitive firms and support rising the prosperity. A context that continuously creates pressure for firms to upgrade the source and sophistication of their advantage, and at the same time, supports the upgrading process is a favorable microeconomic context. Pressure for upgrading is applied by demand conditions featuring sophisticated and demanding customers, whose demands spur the local firms to innovate in order to upgrade their product or service offerings. Particularly valuable is the pressure from local customers who anticipate the nature of demand elsewhere in the world. Different competitors, however, might aim to satisfy three different types of demand—existing, latent, or incipient. Existing demand refers to a product bought to satisfy a recognized need. Latent demand applies in a situation where a particular need has been recognized, but no products have been offered, while incipient demand describes a projected need that will emerge when customers become aware of it sometime in the future.

Many companies would be engaged in the market operations in such market, selling competitive products with marginal differentiation that trigger high substitution effect and increase the bargaining power of consumers toward product preferences in reference to price and promotion. One of the procompany demand situations present in the markets is latent demand when the demand for the products exists, but the products are not available. Companies can take advantage of markets in such destination and enjoy near-monopoly for a short period, as it takes time for the local competition to emerge. Companies can use this near-monopoly market situation to architect brand and set price levels, and deliver adequate customer value to generate the brand loyalty. Most companies exploiting the latent demand realize the first mover advantages and attain market leadership. Companies engaged in manufacturing and marketing of high technology and high-value products often need to create demand by educating the consumers on the prescribed and perceived use values of their products and services. Such demand situation is explained as incipient demand. In the incipient demand, though companies enjoy near-monopoly situation for a short period, the market share grows slowly, as most consumers respond slowly to the experimental products. However, in both latent and incipient demand situations, there is threat of emergence of disruptive technology and products that target to attack the market share of these companies.

In making decision on commercializing the innovations, companies generally carry benefit–cost analysis (BCA) if they feel that the advantages of a particular action are likely to outweigh its drawbacks. In the public arena, formal BCA is sometimes a controversial technique for thoroughly and consistently evaluating the pros and cons associated with prospective policy changes. Specifically, it is an attempt to identify and express in dollar terms, all of the effects of proposed government policies or projects. Benefits in a market are measured by the propensity of consumers to pay for the product and services of the firm. The proper calculation of costs is the amount of compensation required to exactly offset negative consequences. The growing market dynamism, innovation, and technologies have posed new challenges toward the competitive advantage and sustainability of companies in reference to improving productivity, quality, and speed, benchmarking, and reengineering of manufacturing and business processes. As a result, dramatic operational improvements have taken place, but these gains have rarely translated into sustainable profitability. And gradually, the tools have substituted strategy to achieve the competitive advantage by undertaking the careful analysis of the microeconomic environment in the host country. A company's profitability depends partly on the structure of the industry in which it competes.

Industry structure resides in five basic forces of competing: the intensity of rivalry among the existing competitors, the threat of new entrants, the threat of substitute products or services, the bargaining power of suppliers, and the bargaining power of buyers. Industry structure is relatively stable, but industries are sometimes transformed by changes in buyer needs, regulation, or technology. Companies can shape the industry structure rather than passively react to it. Many factors determine the nature of competition, including rivals, the economics of particular industries, new entrants, the bargaining power of customers and suppliers, and the threat of substitute services or products. A strategic plan of action based on this might include: positioning the company so that its capabilities provide the best defense against the competitive forces, influencing the balance of forces through strategic moves, and anticipating shifts in the factors underlying competitive forces (Rajagopal 2016).

References

Baker, T.L., Jr., J.J. Cronin, and C.D. Hopkins. 2009. "The Impact of Involvement on Key Service Relationships." *Journal of Services Marketing* 23, no. 2, pp. 114–23.

Birkinshaw, J., J. Bessant, and R. Delbridge. 2007. "Finding, Forming, and Performing: Creating Networks for Discontinuous Innovation." *California Management Review* 49, no. 3, pp. 67–83.

Bowen, H.K., K.B. Clark, C.A. Holloway, and S.C. Wheelwright. 1994. "Development Projects: The Engine of Renewal." *Harvard Business Review* 72, no. 5, pp. 108–20.

Bruhn, M. 2003. *Relationship Marketing Management of Customer Relationships.* Harlow: Pearson.

Chakravorti, B. 2004. "New Rules for Bringing Innovations to Market." *Harvard Business Review* 82, no. 3, pp. 58–67.

Day, G.S. 1990. *Market Driven Strategy: Process for Creating Value.* New York: Free Press.

Doiron, D. 2015. *What Business is Zara in?* Cambridge, MA: Harvard Business School Press.

Elton, J., and J. Roe. 1998. "Bringing Discipline to Project Management." *Harvard Business Review* 76, no. 2, pp. 78–83.

Frederick, D.M. 1989. "Auditors' Representation and Retrieval of Internal Control Knowledge." Working paper, Boulder, CO: University of Colorado at Boulder.

Goldstein, D.G., E.J. Johnson, A. Herrmann, and M. Heitmann. 2008. "Nudge Your Customers Toward Better Choices." *Harvard Business Review* 86, no. 12, pp. 99–105.

Gulati, R. 2007. "Silo Busting: How to Execute on the Promise of Customer Focus." *Harvard Business Review* 85, no. 5, pp. 98–108.

Hamel, G., and N. Tennant. April 27, 2015. "The 5 Requirements of a Truly Innovative Company." *Harvard Business Review Blog*. Retrieved on April 28, 2016 from https://hbr.org/2015/04/the-5-requirements-of-a-truly-innovative-company

Hulten, B. 2007. "Customer Segmentation: The Concepts of Trust, Commitment and Relationship." *Journal of Targeting, Measurement and Analysis for Marketing* 15, no. 4, pp. 256–69.

Locke, C. 2000. "Smart Customers, Dumb Companies." *Harvard Business Review* 78, no. 6, pp. 187–191.

Payne, A., and P. Frow. 2005. "Strategic Framework for Customer Relationship Management." *Journal of Marketing* 69, no. 4, pp. 167–76.

Rajagopal. 2010. "Bridging Sales and Services Quality Functions in Retailing of High Technology Consumer Products." *International Journal of Services and Operational Management* 6, no. 5, pp. 177–99.

Rajagopal. 2016. *Sustainable Growth in Global Markets: Strategic Choices and Managerial Implications*. Basingstoke, Hampshire, UK: Palgrave Macmillan.

Rayport, J.F., and B.J. Jaworski. 2004. "Best Face Forward." *Harvard Business Review* 82, no. 12, pp. 1–12.

Reeves, M., and M. Deimler. 2011. "Adaptability: The New Competitive Advantage." *Harvard Business Review* 89, no. 7, pp. 135–41.

Saldanha, F.P., and M. Pozzebon. 2015. *Fiat Mio: The Project That Embraced Open Innovation, Crowdsourcing and Creative Commons in the Automotive Industry*. Cambridge, MA: Harvard Business School Press.

Senge, P.M., and G. Carstedt. 2001. "Innovating Our Way to the Next Industrial Revolution." *MIT Sloan Management Review* 42, no. 2, pp. 24–39.

Sharma, A., and J.N. Seth. 1997. "Relationship Marketing: An Agenda for Inquiry." *Industrial Marketing Management* 26, no. 2, pp. 87–89.

Williams, C., and L. Emily. 2014. *3M Taiwan: Product Innovation in the Subsidiary*. Cambridge, MA: Harvard business School Press.

Williamson, P.J., and E. Yin. 2014. "Accelerated Innovation: The New Challenge from China." *MIT Sloan Management Review* 55, no. 4, pp. 1–8.

Wilson, K., and Y.L. Doz. 2012. "10 Rules for Managing Global Innovation." *Harvard Business Review* 90, no. 10, pp. 84–90.

Winter, A., and V. Govindarajan. 2015. "Engineering Reverse Innovations." *Harvard Business Review* 93, nos. 7–8, pp. 80–89.

CHAPTER 3

Setting Up Innovative Business Projects

Overview

For many companies, innovation is a sprawling collection of initiatives, energetic but uncoordinated, and managed with vacillating strategies. Hence, it is necessary for the companies to set up an innovative business project, infusing a systematic process. In order to capitalize on the current and future market opportunities, global, regional, and local companies are investing substantial time and resources in developing innovative business projects that can create sustainable competitive differentiation. The chapter discusses entrepreneurial attributes that are basic to develop and implement innovative business projects, and guides the process of managing resources and project cost rationally. It is a precondition for building and implementing innovative business projects to create a right and sustainable market to absorb the thrust of innovative products. This chapter discusses the ways for market creation and for developing leadership. The most challenging issues in developing nonconventional business projects include tangible and intangible organizational factors like market change management, improvement in the products and services, enhancing customer values, and building task-reporting, monitoring, and evaluation approaches. The lean thinking for implementing innovative business projects' basic project management skills like constituting project teams, setting project charter, and developing performance measures and standards are also discussed in this chapter.

Entrepreneurial Attributes

Innovation has been embedded in the business process of the companies in order to improve their market competitiveness, enhance market leadership, and attain high business performance. However, the major challenge for the companies is to explore the market-oriented and consumer-preferred innovative ideas, and converge them with the project-management process. Innovative ideas, concepts, prototypes, and applications are grown under the entrepreneurial environment within or outside the company. As the innovations today in the business-to-consumer and business-to-business segments have shown a tendency of boom and bust, one of the major concerns for the companies carrying out innovative business projects is to make it competitive and sustainable in the marketplace over the spatial and temporal dynamics. Small start-up enterprises (SUEs) that emerge with new business innovation ideas and projected performance in business often suffer from low entrepreneurial confidence due to cost and time overrun syndrome of innovation, or ending up the innovation in a niche with less obvious performance of the project. Hence, large companies are coming forward to adopt SUEs, build required entrepreneurial attributes among the start-up innovation project teams, monitor the stage-wise performance of the innovation project, and meticulously work out the investment-return ratio on innovative business projects.

In order to reduce redundancy in new product innovation and inconsistency in the innovative business projects, companies sponsoring SUEs often find that the harder they work bringing innovative products into the marketplace and toward improving their manufacturing processes, the greater are the elusive benefits. The principal concern for innovation-driven companies is the assurance to deliver both conceptual and operational benefits to the stakeholders. Conceptual learning addresses the know-why attributes and delivers a better understanding of the cause-and-effect relationships through innovation experience and peer reviews. Operational benefit of an innovation leads to delivering a new or virgin concept to the consumers, with substantial evidence of high satisfaction and returns on investment on the innovation. Innovative business projects that deliver high levels of both learning approaches and operational advantages working with efficient project teams sustain in the global marketplace today (Lapre and van Wassenhove 2002). Innovative business projects become successful, provided they have the right leadership and team approach to manage tasks. An innovative business project needs to be developed with a goal-oriented approach, set knowledge of standards at each stage of the project among the team members, build the ability to manage project financials accurately, and build the competence to manage project risks and contingencies. A project manager should be an innovator who is deeply involved in the innovation project, understanding the concepts and operational path thereof. In addition, the project leader should demonstrate interpersonal skills, management abilities, possess the knowledge about the project environment, and should be thorough in application of innovation benefits among the consumers, stakeholders, and market players.

Innovation Entrepreneurship

Innovation projects in most companies are based on the consumer preferences and the need for competitive differentiation. Accordingly, investments in innovative business projects follow a boom-bust cycle. The contemporary trend shows that the growing SUEs at the bottom-of-the-pyramid of various geo-demographic segments keep analyzing the consumer needs and attempt on co-creating innovative products. These SUEs set their priorities and explore sponsor companies to support research budgets to continue working on the business projects. Sustainable innovation requires a new approach with better initiatives to gain access to the insights and build capabilities for managing innovation alliance with large companies (Wolpert 2002). Establishing innovative business projects for gaining market competitiveness in the global and emerging markets needs team dynamics at the grassroots, financial and human resources for working with innovation projects, and continuous investment in research and development. However, the risk of commercialization of innovation grows simultaneously as the innovative business projects move ahead.

For over a decade, multinational enterprises from developed countries have moved a substantial part of their research and development (R&D) activity to emerging markets such as India and China. As the innovation began sprouting at the low scale in the emerging markets with potential benefits across the larger markets, multinational companies tend to invest in R&D and co-create skilled manpower at low cost. The dynamics of R&D sponsored by the multinational companies are oriented toward customer-centric innovations that involve all market players in exploring new opportunities and challenges. Many SUEs in emerging markets have evolved to develop advanced technical capabilities, and innovative business projects are developed involving multinational companies. However, the thinking on low-cost innovation with capacity building of SUEs in local economic environment is often weak due to the dominant innovation mindset, structures, and unplanned processes. Hence, large companies co-designing and collaborating with the local companies should give a systematic start to innovative business projects by developing mission, goals, objectives, project portfolios, and constructing a WBS. Most of the amateur SUEs lack in such project planning measures and often suffer from the unexpected flaws during the innovation process.

It is necessary for the innovation companies to develop a sustainable framework that can be used by managers in both local and multinational companies to support the key decisions on innovating a new product and build its market competitiveness. The companies engaged in sponsoring innovation R&D in the outfits of potential markets of global, regional, local geo-demographic segments should consider developing technological capability to improve the innovation research in the innovation nurturing enterprises, measure the size of the innovation and uniqueness of the market opportunity, and build capability and competence among the employees of the innovation co-designer and managing companies (Jha et al. 2016). The innovation companies can set clear mission and goals for working with the innovative business projects considering the following attributes:

- Define the innovation project objectives clearly in reference to its market potential and competitiveness.
- Develop a link between their projects and the company's mission, goals, objectives, and strategy.
- Develop the right rationale for undertaking the innovation project, convergence with the innovation enterprises, and setting the time, cost, and outcome of the project.
- Setting mission statement, usually at high level, providing the vision and values for the company.
- List the achievements that the company wishes to accomplish by successfully managing the innovation project.

As the market competition is increasing manifold in the global marketplace, companies in many industries are feeling immense pressure to improve their ability to innovate. A well-defined and comprehensive innovation project with specific statements that the company wishes to achieve might accomplish success, provided the company develops precisely the innovation strategies and competencies with the project team. However, the major crux in investing on the in-company R&D tasks is that the best ideas do not always roll-out of laboratories. Hence, a large number of companies are leaning toward exploring the idea of open-market innovation, an approach that uses tools such as licensing, joint ventures, and strategic alliances, to bring the benefits of free trade to the flow of new ideas (Rigby and Zook 2002). ONergy, a for-profit social enterprise engaged in developing low-cost energy solution for public consumption in India, is based on the renewable energy products. This nonbusiness organization is aiming to scale up its operations for providing electricity at low cost to the underserved consumers in the bottom-of-the-pyramid market segment in India. This start-up organization has two major concerns to commercialize its innovative products—exploring a sponsor to support R&D, and marketing operations, and creating a brand in this market has proved difficult, as competition comprises many large and small players. New innovative products invariably need adequate investment in brand building as a way to ensure better acceptance by consumers and develop appropriate branding strategies. The start-up social enterprises in developing markets are getting engaged in creating unique brands that are strategically profitable in the competitive marketplace (Saikat and Aneja 2014).

The emerging trend across the global market shows that innovations today are largely customer-centric and driven by the users. Customers offer solutions to the companies for commercialization, and in turn, drive companies to deliver innovative tangibles that make competitive differentiation and provide value for money. Generally, SUEs join customers though the social and peer digital networks to explore the embedded preferences and solutions to the existing gaps in the products and services and explore to develop innovative products systematically. The SUEs serve as bidirection information hub between the customers and the companies sponsoring innovative business projects. Customers, in most cases like mobile phone, tablets, photo and video equipment, computers and office equipment, reveal what they want a new product or service to do for them, and the companies need to get the right clue from the customers' experience. In order to converge customer information with the innovative projects, companies should delineate effective steps for capturing, analyzing, and utilizing the customer input. Companies intending to carry out the innovative business projects should also rank the innovations in reference to their importance and desired satisfaction, considering the simple formula described as follows:

$$\mathrm{IBP}_r^{tj} = \frac{\left\{\mathrm{I}_{imp} + \left(\mathrm{I}_{imp} - \mathrm{C}_{sat}\right)\right\}}{\mathrm{I}_{tc}}\left(\mathrm{I}_{ms}^{tj}\right)\cdots \tag{3.1}$$

In the preceding equation:

- IBP_r^{tj} indicates the rank of an innovation business project in a given market "j" at time "t."
- The importance of the product from the perspective of company is denoted by I_{imp} while C_{sat} expresses the score of customer satisfaction.
- The total cost to the company in managing and implementing the innovation projects are indicated by I_{tc}, and I_{ms}^{tj} symbolizes the potential or expected market share of the innovative product in a given market "j" at time "t."

The preceding simple mathematical formula may be used by the companies to get an approximate rank of the selected innovative ideas and projects before setting the innovative business projects. Such exercise on opportunity calculation could help companies learn the relative attractiveness innovative projects and the underlying key opportunities toward investing in the innovation projects (Ulwick 2002).

Innovation entrepreneurship necessarily entails both SUEs and sponsor companies that would be willing to commercialize the innovation. The innovative companies face risk and high levels of uncertainty as the innovation projects move the stages of commercialization and sustainability. Established organizations that intend to manage innovative business projects are typically market-oriented and develop marketing strategies to carry the innovations forward to the consumes as well to the competitive marketplace. Such companies make conscious efforts to build capability and competence among the employees of the organization and develop sustainable entrepreneurship. Commitment to entrepreneurship may cycle between high or moderate support in reference to the conditions in the internal and external environment shift. In order to improve the entrepreneurial capabilities, companies develop strategic objectives to guide entrepreneurs, offer management the structure to support their innovation projects and carry forward the innovation project tasks, and deliver relevant decision support (Kelley 2011). Through an Initiation and Implementation model, as exhibited in Figure 3.1, the innovative business projects are adjusted to the market conditions accordingly in the external environment monitor the progress of the project within the organization. The innovation entrepreneurship is a process that encompasses various backward and forward linkages embedded to the stages of innovative business projects.

Innovation entrepreneurship is a convergence of SUEs and sponsoring companies, which moves from the stage of initiation to the systematic

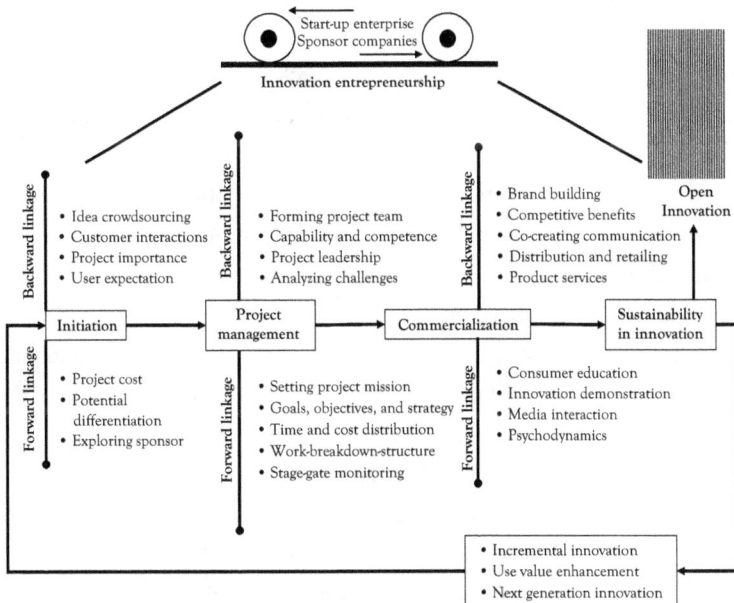

Figure 3.1 Stages and linkages of innovation entrepreneurship

project management to commercialization, and finally developing sustainable innovation through incremental innovations, as illustrated in the Figure 3.1. The backward linkages in the initiation stage of conceiving innovative business project constitute crowdsourcing of ideas, understanding customer needs and preferences, determining the importance of the innovation, and evaluating the expectation of consumers upon implementing the innovation project successfully. The estimated cost of the innovation, its market potential for commercialization, and search for the right sponsor to undertake the innovation project are the major forward linkage tasks to initialize such projects. Upon seeking initial approval to the project by examining various elements at the initiation stage, the innovative project enters into the real project management stage, which demands formation of project teams, training of the team members, developing project leadership, and analyzing challenges in the innovative business projects. These activities form the backward linkages, while setting project mission, goal, objectives, task management strategies constitute the forward linkages besides time and cost management and developing a WBS. One of the most scientific method to monitor progress of the innovative projects is considered to be the stage-gate process that helps managers by assigning tasks in respective stages of the project management and review them as the tasks are completed during the stage. Such project-management approaches check the defects or gaps in task administration at each stage and help managers in avoiding accumulation of defects at the end of the project, which is complex to sort and fix. The major challenges in the stage of commercialization of innovation are brand building through advertising and communication, and developing distribution, retailing, and services for the innovative products. Some innovations are conceived to serve the incipient demand, which needs creation of demand for the product. This appears to be more challenging than serving the innovation products to the existing demand. Companies need to invest substantial resources toward consumer education in order to create consumer demand. Besides, companies also have to carry out product demonstrations such as "do-it-yourself" and adaptive customization by allowing the consumers to use the new products for a reasonable period to determine their value for money. However, the opportunities for open innovation, incremental innovation, and enhancement of the use value of innovative products over the product lifecycle stages finally take the innovation business projects to the initiation stage of the next-generation innovative products.

Entrepreneurial Attributes

Enterprise ecosystems include well-established firms and new ventures that are laid on the maxims of collaboration and competition, and strategic thinking to leverage a firm's resources and capabilities. Strategic thinking and the entrepreneurial activities in an enterprise ecosystem influence one another in a cycle that diffuses and even sparks innovation (Zahra and Nambisan 2012). As awareness among the entrepreneurs about the innovation initiatives is increasing in the emerging markets, the public support to encourage innovation is gearing up, and voluntary organizations are becoming a face in the crowd to nurture local innovation in the global marketplace. For example, *Fundacion Chile*, a private, nonprofit corporation is contributing to technological innovation at the grassroots enterprises in the country and prompting them to develop productive links, add value, and generate technological and human skills to grow innovation at home-economic conditions. This nonprofit organization, based on science and technology has emerged as a leading technology institution recognized nationally and internationally with an objective to help amateur innovation enterprises (Tiffin and Carmona 2004).

Entrepreneurs take initiative to bundle resources in innovative ways and are willing to bear the risk and uncertainty to act. In the increasing market competition and threat of emerging new firms, entrepreneurs must exhibit the following attributes to succeed:

- Continuity in creation or co-creation process
- Investing time and effort in enterprise planning
- Mapping risks and critical success factors in enterprise

To be competitive, companies must grow innovative new businesses. Given the nature of their decision-making environment, entrepreneurs sometimes need to effectuate, be cognitively adaptable, and learn from failure. The effectuation process in enterprise development starts with what one has (who they are, what they know, and whom they know) and selects among the possible outcomes. The entrepreneurial behavior in general is responsive to a judgmental decision under uncertainty about a possible opportunity for profit. Most entrepreneurs think in a casual process to start an enterprise with a desired outcome and focus on the means to generate that outcome.

Most start-up innovation enterprises at the local markets are very fragile due to risk, contingencies, cost, and time overrun in managing new product tasks. Entrepreneurs are not strong enough to face the uncertainties and loss in the innovation, as they are not often disciplined in managing the innovation projects. Although, some SUEs, which are prepared to explore the potential opportunities as well as have the capacity to absorb the risk of failure, might foresee outsized rewards as it entails manifold benefits of commercializing the innovation. The critical success factor in entrepreneurship is embedded in effectively managing the uncertainty while trying something new, independent of its ecosystem. However, believing that every contingency can be anticipated and innovation can be managed without risk might be a larger mistake made by the entrepreneurs. A disciplined approach of entrepreneurship requires to constitute an innovation team, gather awareness about the innovation these, find its ecosystem, estimate cost, time, risk, and marketability of the new innovative product, and finally, explore for a sponsor to work on an innovating business project. Accordingly, an entrepreneur formulates a working hypothesis about an opportunity, assembles the resources to test the hypothesis, and finally designs and runs real-world experiments. Depending on the results of a round of experimentation, the entrepreneur may revise the project and run another experiment close to harvest the value based on the market potential of the new innovative product (Sull 2004).

Entrepreneurship is a not an easy proposition in the competitive marketplace today. New ventures encounter variety of barriers and develop miss-match with the existing marketing systems, processes, and cultures. Nonetheless, the success of small and medium enterprises requires a balance of conventional and new organizational traits. The entrepreneurial challenges appear when the new business is pursued and the market does not respond appropriately to the products, services, and strategies of the firm. Thus, firms must perform the following balancing actions (Garvin and Levesque 2006):

- Develop strategy by trial and error, which includes narrowing potential choices, learning from small samples, using pro- totypes to test business models, tracking progress through nonfinancial measures, and knowing how and when to pull the plug on a new venture.
- Find the best combination of conventional and new opera- tional processes by pooling adequate resources, technology, and manpower.
- Learn meticulously about the capabilities to develop and to acquire, and sharing responsibility for operating decisions.
- Strike the right balance of integration and autonomy by assigning both entrepreneurial and organizational strategies to new ventures and establishing creative think tanks to support the innovative ideation process.

The success factors of an innovation-driven enterprise include careful planning, accuracy in costing, and uniqueness of the project to distinguish the competitive differentiation. Companies can measure the planning and cost indicators in a scale of 1 to 10 to have a clear appraisal of success factors in implementing the innovative business projects. In reference to planning, score 1 indicates being easy to plan while score 10 denotes that the selected innovation is harder to plan and more planning requirements need to be met by the company. Similarly, score 1 for the cost indicator would suggest that the project cost works out to be lower, while score 10 indicates that the project would be very expensive and need enormous capital resources. Accordingly, the companies engaged in the innovation process may decide whether or not to take up such an innovation project. Contrary to these measure of scale, in reference to measuring the unique- ness of the innovation project, score 1 would indicate a highly common project with zero competitive differentiation, suggesting not to work on such innovation project, while score 10 for this measure would indicate that the project is highly unique and exhibits enormous competitive dif- ferentiation to make the innovation project a success. A company may undertake one or more innovation projects based on the available human and capital resources, ability to take risk, and competency in commercializing the innovation projects. Under such circumstances, it is necessary for the companies to develop innovative business projects portfolio and manage them, considering the following project rules:

- Select the number of projects for processing and implementation
- Maintaining a good balance among the project attributes following a score matrix
- Clearly link the projects to mission, goals, and objectives of the company
- Respect the uniqueness and product differentiation for each selected project
- Manage project tasks on market-driven insights and create high consumer awareness about the innovative products
- Develop core competencies in implementing the project
- Inculcate disciplined task execution approach among the members of the project team
- Calculate the payback time the project takes to recover investment
- Work out the net present value of the new product in reference to the current value of returns

In the dynamic marketplace of today, entrepreneurs must move quickly as opportunity may no longer exist. Entrepreneurs should understand that the competitive marketplace today is complex and demonstrates ingenuity, spontaneity, and hustle. Profitable survival of new enterprises requires an edge derived from some combination of a creative idea and a superior capacity for execution. Effective entrepreneurs filter unpromising ideas as early as possible through judgment and reflection and do not depend on gathering lots of data to screen out the nonexecutable and unprofitable decisions. Good entrepreneurs assess realistically their financial resources, personal and organizational preferences, and goals for the firm. To ensure the right utilization of time and money, successful entrepreneurs also optimize the resources use and minimize the occurrence of flaws in production, marketing, and operations processes (Bhide 1994). However, with every enterprise, the major issue remains about the marketing of the innovative product by determining the right price point in a consumer market that is trendy and consumers would be willing to pay. Upon observing the market test results of the innovative product, most enterprises lean toward cutting back on differentiating features to reduce costs and engineer the product to an acceptable cost of goods and retail price point. For example, an entrepreneur Gauri Nanda had conceived a new idea of roll-away alarm clock—Clocky and launched the product under the aegis of Nanda Home. Clocky is the alarm clock on wheels that runs away beeping. It can be snoozed one time, but if the master of the clock does not get up, Clocky will jump off of the nightstand up to 3 feet high, and run around the room. Having achieved commercial success with the first product Clocky of Nanda Home, the innovative team of the enterprise interacted with the consumers to architect the new products functionally and emotionally appealing. After launching two more extensions of the Clocky line, the team has been engaged in designing, developing, and marketing another consumer product that would solve an everyday problem with lifelike charm and position it using psychographic strategies for consumers of all ages and gender (Ofek 2013).

The review of the available literature suggests that the marketing theory and entrepreneurial theory have evolved simultaneously. The successful entrepreneurs develop their business strategies around the market to accomplish the following objectives:

- To provide the best offer to the market
- Discover better solutions to the buyers' needs at lower costs than the competitors
- Create outstanding customer value
- Develop consumer-, market-, and product-oriented strategies
- Execute transactional and relational marketing-oriented strategies in the competitive marketplace

The entrepreneurs are largely driven by a vision to create value to customers and earn profit through their applied entrepreneurial skills and customer-centric marketing actions. Entrepreneurship and marketing theories share some commonality as both disciplines focus on identify-ing the opportunities and transforming resources into value-creation or co-creation for consumers. Successful entrepreneurs follow an effectuate route in entrepreneurship (Sarasvathy 2001). Entrepreneurs carry out thinking and continuous efforts to improve customer value, may be better off than what is prescribed in the traditional market theories. This attri-bute exhibits a better fit between the external market conditions and the internal environment in which the market decisions are made. Influence from entrepreneurship allows understanding the parts of modern market behavior better and analyzing the cognitive dimensions of entrepreneurs. The attributes of exploring opportunities and identifying the suitable one for doing business is also a symmetrical process in both marketing and entrepreneurship. In principal, opportunities are identified through mar-ket analyses in traditional marketing theory. Within entrepreneurship, this is regarded as a much more complicated process and can be regarded as an important part of the value-creating process (Hills, Hansen, and Hultman 2005). Entrepreneurial activities are an important part of today's business world, and this should be reflected in how we teach and research marketing. The interface between entrepreneurship and market-ing creates prolific business developments for marketing such as oppor-tunity recognition processes, decision making and implementation, and strategic marketing (Hultman and Hills 2011). Market entrepreneurship has developed strongly as a result of the increasing global competition and is aimed at introducing novelty, innovation, or arbitrage into the production and exchange processes. Thus, the governments of develop-ing countries stimulate productive entrepreneurship and make enterprises practical and operational through various public policies. The attributes and ecosystem of entrepreneurial mindset to work with innovation proj-ects is exhibited in Figure 3.2.

There are two phases of the entrepreneurial mindset that demonstrate cognitive acceptance or cognitive dissonance in undertaking the innova-tion initiatives, as shown in the Figure 3.2. Most entrepreneurs catch up with the innovative ideas accidentally, while in social interactions than through a planned search for an innovative theme and measure their capa-bility and competence to proceed with the innovation process, during which they also seek the support of government and society. One of the

Project development
- Constituting team
- Estimating cost
- Time span
- Setting goals and objectives

- Entrepreneurial desire
- Capability and competence
- Innovation ideas
- Leadership
- Social leverage

The ground

- Information analysis
- Idea selection
- Confidence building
- Cognitive drive

Initiation

The challenges
- Resources
- Operational risk
- Time and cost overrun
- Marketability

Cognitive
acceptance

Growth of
innovation
and shift in
market behavior

The support
- Empowerment
- Government policies
- Resources management
- Project governance

The dynamics
- Family and culture
- Exploring sponsor
- Innovation blueprint
- Past experience
- Decision making

Experimentation
- Open innovation
- Radical moves
- Reverse innovation
- Low cost-niche led ideas

Threats
- Market failures
- Sunk cost
- Risk rollout
- Competition
- Aborting project

Cognitive
dissonance

Entrepreneurial mindset

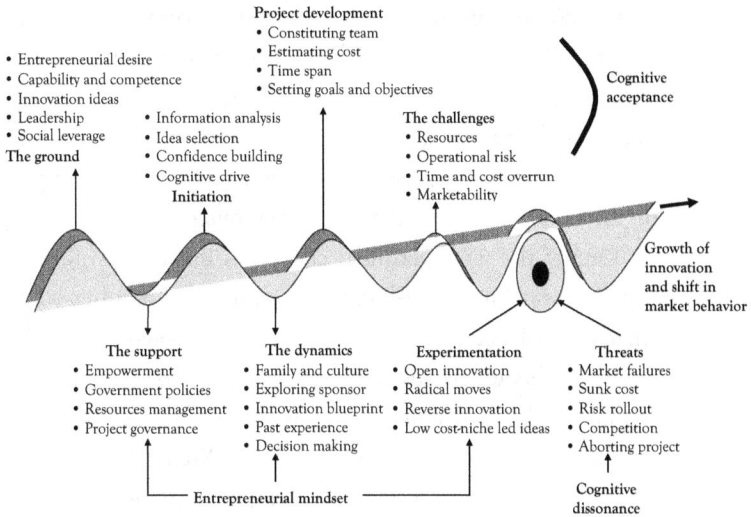

Figure 3.2 Entrepreneurial mindset and the innovation project path

major challenges in the conventional social and cultural environment is the empowerment of entrepreneurs that builds confidence among the innovators to inculcate a proinnovation cognitive drive. Entrepreneurs need to scrutinize enormous personal and professional information of the interested people to induct into the innovation project and constitute appropriate teams. Besides driving the innovation project through the challenges of managing the resources efficiently, handling operational risk, marketability, and cost and time overrun, entrepreneurs often face market failures and piling up of sunk cost due to radical and experimental innovation approach. Such endeavors cause risk roll-outs though out the project, leading to abort the innovation untimely, which develops serious cognitive dissonances among entrepreneurs (Bettencourt and Bettencourt 2011).

Entrepreneurship also runs in the family businesses. Firms desiring on continuously generative returns on investment and increasing margin of profit cannot rely on either strategy or entrepreneurship alone, but instead must successfully engage in strategic entrepreneurship. However, profitable niches evolve, shift, and disappear rapidly in the competitive market economy. Thus, some firms focus solely on entrepreneurial strategy, which might become an effective tool to sustain market competition in the long run. Without an effective strategy to create competitive advantage in pursuing these entrepreneurial opportunities, a firm will soon experience imitation by competitors whose offerings will erode its profits. Entrepreneurship begins with an appropriate mindset based on the right decisions on exploring and exploiting the opportunities. The balance of exploration and exploitation results in the key outcome of continuous innovation. One of the most pertinent challenges involved in pursuing strategic entrepreneurship is developing an appropriate mindset within the firm that can balance short- and long-term entrepreneurial objectives. A mindset refers to the cognitive frameworks through which new and existing knowledge is interpreted and used to inform decisions such as those regarding strategy and entrepreneurship (Webb, Ketchen, and Ireland 2010). The innovation entrepreneurship, which grows in the family business, largely operates in a niche as such entrepreneurs are not pro-open innovation. The entrepreneurial focus in a family-run environment does not always stay progressive; it is rather confined into a streamlined segment with low commercial vigor. The family-based innovation enterprises establish good governance practices that separate the family and the business and ensure oversight from a professional board and are careful not to lose the product uniqueness and the brand reputation woven around the *family gravity*. Such enterprises grow innovation leadership within the family values and learned competencies (Fernandez, Iqbal, and Ritter 2015).

The entrepreneurial thinking process demands continuous flow of new ideas. The ideas for innovations are the precious currency of the new market economy, but their generation is a mysterious process. Businesses that constantly innovate have systematized the production and testing of new ideas, and the system can be replicated by practically any organization. The best innovators use old ideas as the raw materials for new ideas. Entrepreneurs need to develop their thinking process in the following way:

- Nurture good ideas from a wide variety of sources
- Keep those ideas alive by steering, discussing among peers, and applying them in niche environments

- Visualize new uses of conventional wisdom and encourage cross-pollination of thoughts within the organization that allow peer interactions
- Turn promising concepts into real services, products, processes, or business models to gain competitive advantage in the market

Leading entrepreneurs may use the aforementioned thought process to generate innovative strategies. Most dynamic enterprises tend to move new ideas from one market to another and intend to build full-fledged consulting groups to refine the thought process and internal knowledge on entrepreneurial leadership by innovations. The most important issue in cultivating such thought process is to strike a balance between the organizational responsiveness to the innovating thinking and organizational work culture (Keidel 2013). Entrepreneurial mindset involves the ability to rapidly sense, act, and mobilize even under uncertain conditions. Most entrepreneurs learn in a dual-process way. This process suggests two-level interactive learning platforms based on the idea of the interaction by means of explicit and implicit learning through reinforcement. It accounts for many unexplained cognitive perceptions and phenomena based on casual and peer interactions. There are many applied implications of the dual-learning process, leading to the following attributes among entrepreneurial thinking process:

- Entrepreneurs acquire knowledge through feelings and reactions as experienced in real situations
- Realizing that the psychological and physiological outcomes caused by the feelings of loss of the right thought process are symptoms in the innovation process may reduce secondary sources of stress among entrepreneurs
- There is a process of recovery to learn from failure, which offers some comfort that the current feelings of loss will eventually diminish
- The recovery and learning processes can be enhanced by some degree of co-creation or peer interactions

- Recovery from loss offers an opportunity to increase one's knowledge of entrepreneurship and regenerate the thinking process

There is often an imbalance between the flow of ideas and implementing them to get solutions in a growing entrepreneurial firm. Entrepreneurs face with a problem in fitting the ideas to resolve the complexes in innovation and growth, so most entrepreneurs jump immediately to focusing on crash solutions, devoting little time to analyze why the problem exists in the first place. This is one of the flaws in traditional thinking, which may lead to conclusions without any rationale. In the marketplace today, consistent thinking for continuous innovation becomes increasingly important for the simple reason that the challenges enterprises face are becoming more complex (May 2012).

The SUEs are sensitive to the utilization of capital resources, managing liquidity, and carrying the innovation projects at the economies of scale. Most innovation enterprises at the stage of initiation set a narrow scope, but if their project outcome has the potential for commercialization of innovation, large corporations lean toward sponsoring the project and planning long into the future of innovation management. Good SUEs pursue 4Cs comprising continuity, community, connection, and command, turning these features into sources of distinction and competitive advantage. The 4C principles grow in every proprietary firm, large or small, or family-owned firms that flourish over generations (Miller and le Breton-Miller 2015).

Every small idea of an entrepreneur may be a powerful means to initiate a business revolution by putting the organization first to acquire market and achieve customer value. Putting the customer first has sparked a revolution at Hindustan Computers Limited, the services giant of India in information technology. This company banked upon the conventional wisdom of valuing the customers first, then turned the hierarchical pyramid upside down by making the management accountable to the employees. By catalyzing both the employees and customers, the emerging enterprise may be able to pave a path of transformation through innovation to enable the firm to grow fast and stay profitable among the competing firms. Entrepreneurs may create a sense of urgency for innovative thinking in the organization by enabling the employees to realize the need for change and inculcate a culture of trust by pushing the transparency in communication and information sharing. Enterprises can grow as a think tank like Toyota and General Electric by developing a bottom-up organizational hierarchy and enabling the ideation process and functions accountable to the employee as performance indicators (Nayar 2010).

Seasoned enterprises in the marketplace know that the opportunities for competitive advantage lie in market muddle, but they recognize the need for developing critical strategic processes. In a traditional strategy, most entrepreneurs derive advantage by exploiting resources and stable market positions for the products and services of their firms. A simple rule of strategy implementation suggests that advantage on outcome appears upon successfully seizing the opportunities. Most firms found good innovation opportunities toward key strategic processes, such as product innovation, partnering, or spinout creation. They need to create simple rules in the innovation process to help managers in pursuing such opportunities in reference to how-to work on innovations, market limitations, priority rules, scheduling, and exit rules. Entrepreneurial firms must follow the set rules meticulously to avoid distraction in the innovation process by changing them frequently. A consistent strategy helps entrepreneurs and managers in sorting out the promising opportunities and gain short-term advantage by exploiting them (Eisenhardt and Sull 2001).

Resource and Cost Management

The major challenge with the innovation companies is managing the human and capital resources efficiently. The fallacy of most innovative business projects is that more resources and cost involvement in an innovation project would lead to a wider and sustainable outcome. Small innovation projects are set with low human and capital resources that often face the serious disorder of cost overruns in the middle of the project as they are unable to manage the resources efficiently. One of the major tasks in managing the human resources is to generate sustainable value from the employees of the company, and more specifically, within the project team. It has been observed by analyzing the performance of innovation-driven companies that they perform at a higher level when they have clear job description, flow of directions, systematic performance appraisal and reporting system, and integrated talent management programs that are aligned with business strategy and project operations. Organizations can get more from their investments by managing human resources in the innovation-driven enterprises. Task allocation and performance management at various stages of the innovation projects are typically based on individual accountability than the collaborative team work. Human resources management practices tend to focus on individual competencies and experiences, entrepreneurial culture, and organizational design. Companies engaged in handling innovative business projects continuously should measure the employee performance periodically for the purpose of work force planning and networking broader collaborative contributions with other innovation management enterprises. Developing innovation networks or innovation consortium including SUEs reveal a significant strength of human resources. Companies nurture innovation networks through talent management initiatives and systematic task allocation in carrying out innovative business projects like organizations including IDEO, IKEA, Dow Chemical, and Best Buy (Schweer et al. 2012).

The most efficient entrepreneurial design in managing innovative business projects would be to develop a team culture and flexible decision making, and reporting organizational design. Such an enterprise system would provide adequate space for everyone to express ideas, develop concepts, design prototypes, and work with the commercialization of innovation projects. Most innovation nurturing organizations that follow top-down hierarchical structure often suffer from performance monitoring and reporting conflicts in the workplace.

In addition to issues of company structure and strategic decision making process, conflicts are set atop of the other questions that include what role the employees need to play to create the stakeholder value control—a scarce resource. A good innovation enterprise should build up the company by acquiring and retaining highly skilled employees, find a way to embed individual-based knowledge in the company, share knowledge across the working teams, and create an engaging, motivating, and bonding culture to attract and keep talented employees and the bonding task for managing innovation projects uninterruptedly (Bartlet and Ghoshal 2002).

Cost Management

It is the fact of market today that sustaining innovation is crucial for a long-term business performance of the company. However, the most significant question in sustaining innovation is the cost surge over the product refinement and extensions. But truly innovative products often ignore costs, like products from Apple Inc., which focus on the customers use value over the concerns on cost of innovation and price competitiveness in the market. However, most innovation management companies are serious about lowering the cost of innovation process in order to stay price-competitive in the market upon launching the product. Controlling cost in the innovation process has one conventional thumb rule to control the time overrun in all stages of the innovation process, right from initiation till the launch of the finished product. The innovation enterprises have adopted the new path of cost reduction through outsourcing the critical tasks in the innovation process that demand larger flow of capital and resources. McDonald's, IKEA, and GE require potential innovators to lead cross-functional teams in developing promising ideas, and then present those ideas to senior management and manage the cost overrun, spillover cost, and curb the sunk costs in the innovation process. Some companies insist that they do a stint in the sales department by developing breakthrough innovators to mentor and manage peer networks to diffuse the innovation at low cost. The escalated cost of marketing also pulls down the price competitiveness of the innovative products. Thus, companies tend to control the marketing costs besides the innovation processing costs by lowering the innovation diffusion costs, reducing the expenditure on advertising, sales, and promotions. The innovations are, thus, made better known to the consumers over the social networks and virtual stores rather than from a television commercial or a billboard. Pushing the innovations to the market through the digital networks appears to be a cost-effective strategy for most enterprises. Practices like these keep companies open to new ideas and prepare them to respond nimbly to innovation (Cohn, Katzenbach, and Vlak 2008).

Commonly all entrepreneurs know that business growth does not just agglomerate, but springs from continuous innovation and improvements over the existing products and services. However, it is usually believed that companies must spend profligately on innovation-related research and development. Most companies are following the austerity measures and reducing the overhead costs in innovation management. In order to manage the costs involved in innovation projects, conscious companies tend to increase the number of innovators or team strength and reduce the time for innovation, so that the product can be launched in the market quickly and the returns on investment can be generated at a faster pace. These companies also focus on developing customer-centric but radical ideas to achieve the competitive differentiation at low cost and uphold the customer value and expectations. Companies with cost effective goals of carrying out innovations for commercialization look for innovation sources outside the organization, and outsource various tasks related to the innovation project. Increase in the learning from small, low-risk experiments, and commitment to long-term, consistent development efforts are encouraged by the innovation-driven companies in order to keep the costs low and increase the returns on investment (Hamel and Getz 2004). The outsourcing market has matured since 1990s, and innovation organizations have begun to examine how external organizational bonding on manufacturing or marketing process can not only achieve cost savings, but also enable innovation in the dynamic business environment. Most managers use the discounted cash flow (DCF) model to help them make decisions such as where to locate a new manufacturing plant or whether to use a foreign or domestic supplier. But DCF typically undervalues flexibility, and as a result, companies may end up with low-cost production as long as everything proceeds according to the plan, but any deviations from the WBS of the project plan might turn highly expensive (de Treville and Trigeorgis 2010).

Standard accounting techniques such as break-even accounting would provide an opportunity for the enterprise on managing checks and balances in order to monitor the performance of innovation projects. However, such approach may not help the companies in reducing the fixed and variable overhead expenses that are responsible for escalation of innovation cost and affecting profits. Besides cost analysis, simplifying the manufacturing process and fixing production matching with the potential demand for the new products is followed by some companies as the best way to ensure return on investment (Woodward 1976). The SUEs as well as R&D organizations in the health care sector in India have developed three powerful organizational advantages as a "hub-and-spoke" configuration of assets, an innovative way of determining the task allocation in an innovation project, and a focus on cost-effectiveness rather than just cost cutting (Govindarajan and Ramamurti 2013). The hub-and-spoke paradigm is a system of connections arranged like a wire wheel, linking the wheel along spokes connected to the hub at the center. The model is advised for managing innovation projects by connecting the project team (hub) with the project charter that delineates the cost, time, risk, deliverables, profitability, stakeholder value, and many other key performance indicators (spokes). This model is commonly used in transport and telecommunications industry.

Work Breakdown Structure

A company working with innovation projects can manage the cost effectiveness throughout the project by developing a clear WBS. In project management and systems engineering, WBS is a deliverable-oriented decomposition of a project with time and task plans fragmented into smaller components. Such division of tasks within a product path allows the companies to set controls over the fixed and variable costs. Deconstructing a large job over time and the cost span into a series of manageable tasks helps managers achieve their goals within the budgetary provisions of the project. Operating within WBS would help companies avoid the supplementary budget requirements and arrange project deliverables within the prescribed time frame. The WBS visually defines the scope into manageable blocks of tasks that a project team can manage within its capability and competence. The WBS incorporates work packages for each task and estimates the cost for each task to be carried out within the estimated project time. The WBS is embedded with the following attributes:

- Work packages
  - Costs and activity durations
  - Size of the work
  - Project cost accounting
  - Control accounts
  - Detailed description of work and technical documentation
- Cost estimates
  - WBS code
  - Milestone
  - Accountability
  - Cost

The work packages should include activity-wise cost and time to task, and the packages should be proportionate to the manpower and time involved in tasks. Such time-task calculation would determine the size of the work and cost approximations. As the work and cost are divided per unit, it is easy for the project team to control the accounts. The cost estimates are generally denoted by the WBS codes that make the project team easy to monitor the task-by-task cost performance and fix the accountability of team members toward managing the cost and time effectiveness. Often projects fail due to inappropriate WBS documentation and management thereof. Figure 3.3 depicts a model WBS and associated control features in an innovation project.

The attributes of WBS and cost and works management in an innovation project are illustrated in Figure 3.3. The project team creates the project WBS by identifying the major functional deliverables and subdividing those deliverables into smaller systems and subdeliverables. These subdeliverables are further decomposed until they turn manageable by a member of the team and accountability can be fixed. The work package represents the list of tasks to be performed by the specific unit of work. From the perspective of controlling costs, these work packages are usually grouped and assigned to a specific department or team to perform. By integrating the cost and work functions from the project's WBS, the organization can track financial progress in addition to project performance.

The WBS provides the framework for organizing and managing the work in smaller deliverables through the predetermined "work packages."

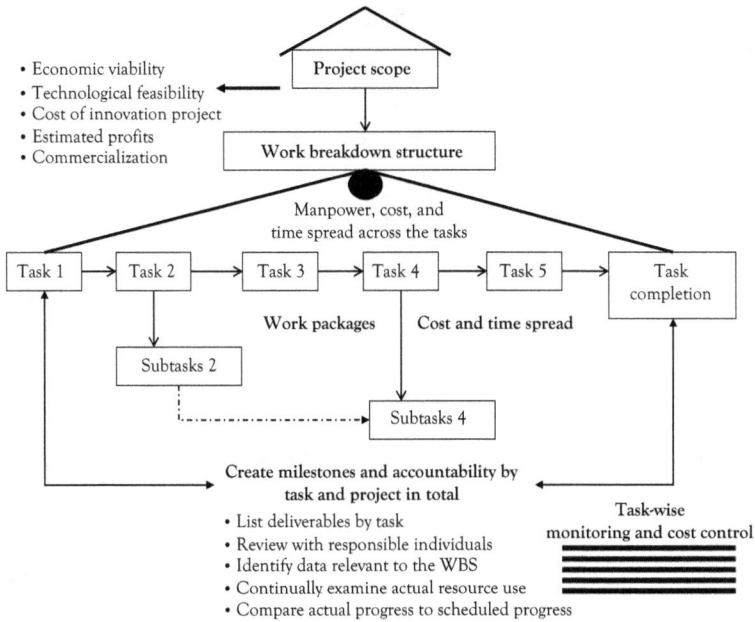

Figure 3.3 Attributes of work breakdown structure

The summary of the WBS identifies the key deliverables that the project should provide and assess deliverables on each work packages. Without WBS, a project would appear too broad and lack in the focus to perform the tasks accurately. The work packages of the project need to be appropriately placed in the project matrix by constituting the project team and led by the competent project manager. As the project is deemed fit to the goals, the WBS is formed in reference to the available resources with the project. The WBS will be expanded to include exactly the type of work that needs to be done working closely with the client and getting what is wanted out of the project into the WBS. By this phase, the actual work on the project is turned on.

Market Development for Innovative Projects

The process of globalization and networking of companies and markets on the global platform began with fierce strategies in the mid-20th century. The shift in the corporate governance and business philosophies among the multinational companies across the world has driven the process of globalization and creation of the concept of global markets. The transformation of business philosophy from "marketing to customer" to "marketing with customer" has triggered the business emotions among the companies to develop customer-centric marketing strategies in order to conquer the high- and low-end markets. As multinational companies of the western hemisphere tend to penetrate into the developing regions and the bottom-of-the-pyramid market segments in search for growth, they have no choice but to compete in the big emerging markets of Brazil, Russia, India, China, Indonesia, and South Africa. The dynamism for globalization has been spread across the political thinkers and business managers hitting dual perspectives of building diplomatic relation by narrowing down trade and economy barriers across the countries in the world and equalizing the power play among the nations, and given more space for multinational companies to do business in the far reachable markets. Although globalization has driven bidirectional efforts of multinational and local companies to share their marketplace in the home and destination countries, still the common question as how these companies play smart to gain the competitive advantage and grow sustainably in the given marketplace persists. During the 1980s, multinationals gained the first-mover advantage in the emerging markets and developed meticulously every element of their business. Some companies believe that they could gain competitive advantage as the emerging markets would merely be new markets for their old products models, and penetrated with an imperialist mindset. But the strategies developed with such thinking narrowed down the success of multinational companies in most emerging markets like India and China that appeared to be innovative in bringing new products at low cost in the market against the multinational companies. Thus, going global has turned a big challenge for the multinational companies, and to evolve in the new marketplace, several critical questions remained to be resolved. Some of them include:

- Who is in the emerging target in the emerging markets— affluent, middle, or bottom-of-the-pyramid market segment?
- How do the distribution and logistics networks operate?
- What mix of local and global leadership is necessary to foster business opportunities?

- Should there be a consistent strategy for doing business in a new marketplace or diverse marketing strategies need to be employed to serve the niches?
- Should there be global-local partnerships promoted to seek a win-win market share in the local markets?

In order to compete in the big emerging markets, companies need to reconfigure their strategies by ascertaining appropriate responses on the competitive fitness and redesign cost and operational dynamics (Prahalad and Lieberthal 2003). It is observed that though the premium consumer segment may attract the companies with global vision, the bottom-of-the-pyramid market appears to be more promising from the perspectives of building the brand equity and customer-centric posture of the company. Companies entering into the premium segment may push themselves to a high-profile niche, but this segment might not support the objective of increasing the market share and staying at par with the mass customers. The new commercial reality is the emergence of omni-presence of global companies across the consumer segments, and leaning toward marketing more standardized products and services than offering customized products on a previously unimagined scale of magnitude. The marketing technology for global, multidomestic, and transnational companies today is to move to digital platforms and give consumers the convenience and cost advantages over the conventional wisdom of laying nonflexible marketing standards. The companies with global standardized products enjoy the benefits of economies of scale in production, distribution, marketing, and advanced management in reference to functional, reliable, and price competitiveness (Levitt 1983).

Breaking the social, cultural, economic, and political barrier for moving the business in various destination markets is a tough challenge for the multinational companies. Though globalization of business has become the lifeline of most companies, creating a sustainable corporate strategy in tune to the local market conditions is difficult. Thus, most companies do not stay competitive in the local markets and lose their market share to the low-cost customer-centric companies. Multinational companies largely employ natives in the destination countries to inculcate the cross-cultural organizational behavior that can enable the company to compete on a worldwide basis, without straying far from headquarters. One of the effective inspirations for foreign companies is the implications of the comparative advantages on factors of products comprising land, labor, capital, workplace talent, and technology, which drive the companies to perform effectively. Overseas companies tend to meet the demands for local convergence and build distinctive competitiveness (Kogut 1999).

There have been many notions on globalization of business comprising various social, economic, political, and ethnic points of views. However, from the perspective of empowering people to access the global markets, demand for products and services has been identified as crystallization of the world as a single place and as the emergence of the global human needs (Robertson 1987). Integration of various digital socioeconomic communication platforms explains that globalization is a reflexive process, and it brings the global markets on one boundary-less play field. The development of new technology allows mass media to become universally available to consumers, and this combines with the cross-border marketing opportunity for the multinational companies (Ritzer 2007). These market trends lead to a homogenization of consumer needs and develop proinnovation and overseas cultures in the emerging markets through new consumption trends, standardization, intercultural collaboration and coordination, and cross-border competition (Zou and Cavusgil 2002). Consistent with the globalization trend, many international companies begin to utilize a global approach, in which companies market their products on a global basis to take the place of the traditional multidomestic approach, in which local subsidiaries market local products to the local markets (Kotabe and Helsen 2010).

Many factors are driving the world toward greater globalization. These factors include the rise of worldwide networks for investment, production, and marketing, advances in telecommunication technologies and the Internet, increase in world travel, and the growth of global media (Yu, Byun, and Lee 2013). Globalization involves the homogenization of international markets and an increasing similarity in the needs and habits of international customers. Using globalized strategies can help international companies create consistent brand images worldwide and use their resources more efficiently. However, any attempt to globally standardize service delivery may encounter difficulties, and it may be argued that every market is unique, and a globalized approach cannot adequately take account of the cultural differences in ethnic markets (Alden, Steenkamp, and Batra 1999). Some leading multinational consumer products companies like Unilever have leaned toward a localized approach, based on the continued desire for maintaining local culture. Indeed, it is clear that many people prefer local consumption imagery, because they can more easily identify with local lifestyles, values, and attitudes. Some studies suggest that neither consumption nor marketing can be made globally uniform. These studies emphasize the powerful influence of local cultures, and demonstrate how customers are developing hybrid cultures or growing with global and local cultural influences (Steenkamp and De Jong 2010).

Most companies also experience a countervailing trend as many consumers seek unique services that reflect their local cultures, lifestyles, and customs. In response, some companies have begun to design their business strategies to fit the special needs and distinct tastes of consumers in particular regions. This localized management approach requires international companies to invest large amounts of time and resources for R&D in an effort to better understand and respond to specific local markets. Companies moving into mass markets and bottom-of-the-pyramid markets in the developing countries grow with localized strategies in different regions (Liu et al. 2014). In view of the experiences of many companies engaged in market expansion amidst the thriving market competition at both the high-end and low-end markets, it may be argued that the globalization of consumer preferences does not necessarily imply convergence in management practices. Globalization (or convergence) and localization (or divergence) are two extremes in the formation of company strategies. Companies often find themselves somewhere in the middle, on the continuum between these two extremes (Yu, Byun, and Lee 2013).

Evolution of the market at the lower end of the global markets is identified as a set of localization processes through which the forces of globalization move in the destination markets (Hansen 2002). The success of McDonald's, Pepsi-Cola, Coca-Cola, and so on is based on variation, that is not offering the same products everywhere around the world, which evidences that globalization does penetrate into the local markets and acquires them or threatens competition to the local firms but in a curious way contributes to its revitalization. For example, take a view at the Cadbury's expansion into the Chinese market as an experiment to investigate whether a company needs to modify its products, production process, product names, and other factors to compete in a new local market (Wood and Grosvenor 2003). Similarly, the chain of small convenience stores, the Seven-Eleven Group, has marked the global success, as the result shows that the success is largely dependent on the company's localized strategies. These cases emphasize the continued desire of customers to maintain their local culture, because people in different markets have different goals, needs, uses for products, and ways of living (Steenkamp and De Jong 2010). The concept of glocalization is a hybrid strategy that embraces elements of global culture and integrates them into the local culture. Robertson has developed the term *glocalization* to explain that global forces do not override locality, and heterogeneity in consumption is an important feature of the modern society (Robertson 1995).

The process of localization of global companies has emerged as the penetration of the global marketing strategies into ethnic business across the wide range of products and preferences, causing rapid business growth for the global firms in different geo-demographic consumer segments. For example, McDonald's uses hybrid, glocalized approaches to incorporate local food preferences and lifestyles by serving spicy cottage cheese burgers in India, beer in The Netherlands, and wine in France (Alden, Steenkamp, and Batra 2006). Management experts in favor of glocalization argue that consumers often draw their preferences, blending the available global and local, and continental and traditional information. Consumers use products to position themselves in the local age, gender, social class, religion, and ethnic hierarchies (Ger and Belk 1996).

Going global seemed to be a glamorous vision for every company in the world till the end of the 20th century. However, the political ideology in the 21st century moved to meticulously develop a global market platform in all destinations by driving cooperation between the domestic and international companies for ensuring mutual business growth of the companies and national economic development. But there are many incidences of multinational companies cannibalizing the market share of local companies and positing economic threats to the country in terms of money laundering, disrupting primary consumer markets, and causing national security concerns. Accordingly, governments of most developing countries have raised the concept of guarded globalization to protect economic, consumer, and national security. Such concern has prompted the developing countries to improve their stakes in the public sector industries. Indeed, the rise of state capitalism in some of the world's most important emerging markets has altered the playing field. Multinational companies must understand globalization's new risks, but project their strategic importance to the host government and their home government and play safe to enter in the destination markets by developing alliances with local players, exploring new ways to add value abroad, and expand business in multiple sectors both at home and overseas destination (Bremmer 2014).

Chaos in market is commonly caused due to congestion of competitors, frequent introduction and withdrawal of products and services, and extensive price promotions. Small differences yield widely diverging outcomes in dynamic market systems, often rendering long-term prediction impossible, in general, in a market or a business. This happens even though the market systems are deterministic, meaning that their future behavior is fully determined overruling the uncertainties. In consumer markets, the chaos is frequent, and these markets are very susceptible to the butterfly effects. The chaos and butterfly effects are very popular in fashion products and consumer electronics. The preceding figure illustrates that the success of any innovation, which has been target for the mass market, may trigger the market chaos as fierce competition begins at the low-end markets. Such competition would divert consumers from the principal brands and acquire them for low-price utilitarian or social status products. The growth of virtual channels would also drive the competition and chaos in the market. The market chaos at the low-end markets is generally prompted by the local companies, which gives way to the international and virtual companies to push through the market space. On the contrary, chaos in the high-end market occurs due to the rush of identical products by high-priced brand icons. Such competition at the high-end markets fragments the market share of companies and drives most consumers to adapt to the fashion consumption behavior, without developing loyalty for any brand. Many firms that enter with one-touch technology fall into the high-end market chaos.

Chaotic market behavior is predictable for a while and then it appears to become random, driving consumers in a dilemma to respond to the uncertain marketing strategies of the companies. The amount of time for which the behavior of market chaos can be effectively predicted depends on what is the tolerance limit of uncertainties in the market, how accurately market dynamism and chain causes and effects can be measured, and how effectively a temporal and spatial scale can be created to monitor and control the market uncertainties in a given time. Chaos in the market is often initiated by the companies that would like to have a leap-frog experience in competition by earning higher market share, applying price-driven tactics. Companies under such market conditions experience high uncertainties and are unable to develop strategic plans. Thus, embracing chaos seems the opposite of discipline and planning. However, uncertainty is embedded in negotiations, and the negotiators who ignore this fact and follow rigid strategies blind themselves to unexpected threats and slip potential opportunities (Wheeler 2004).

Lean Thinking in Innovation Projects

Lean management is a contemporary practice in managing innovative business projects, which allows the companies to establish significant control over the cost spread across the various tasks in a project. The lean practice also permits reduction in inventory levels across the backward and forward supply chains, which results in better financial performance as companies achieve simultaneous declines in manufacturing and service costs. However, lean transformations generally have short-term adverse impacts on the company's bottom line, and managers need to anticipate these challenges and fix them at the earliest before it damages the system and the project performance. Innovation companies may overcome the financial hurdles using the lean management by the value-stream accounting approach, which helps managers to plan for the short-term financial impact, monitor progress, understand the operational improvements, and develop strategies to maximize the longer-term benefit. The lean management approach also replaces the traditional cost-accounting system with a transparent accounting system that tracks the company's value streams, which incorporate all of the value-adding and nonvalue-adding activities required in managing the innovation projects from start to finish (Cooper and Maskell 2008).

Conventionally, companies draw innovation-based projects for a longer time frame, anticipating the risks and contingencies during the project period. Only some preinnovation projects with guaranteed commercial success, go into stealth mode to develop their offerings. Lean startups, in contrast, begin by searching for a business model for each innovation project as they test, revise, and discard task and time overlaps, continually review the performance of each stage of innovation, gathering customer feedback upon commercializing the product, and rapidly iterating on and re-engineering their products. This strategy greatly reduces the chances of the startups spending a lot of time and money in launching products that no one actually will pay for. The SUEs that follow the lean innovation management approach could commence their projects quickly and successfully by reducing the incidence of aborting the project before completion (Blank 2013). The lean strategy process ensures that startups innovate in a disciplined fashion, so that they make the most of their limited resources. Lean strategy helps company builders choose viable opportunities, stay focused, and align the entire organization. The lean process requires setting the vision, defining the firm's near-term goals for success, scope of justifying the goals of the company, and competitive advantage describing the strategies of the company to win the market (Collies 2016).

Constituting Project Teams

"Team" conceptualizes a group of people engaged in delivering a common task. In ideal situations, the individual and group behavior in a team is integrated toward the common objectives and the task delivery process is shared, which leads to set the group dynamics. The basic attributes of a good team include clear identification of goals, clarity of roles, common feeling, motivation, commitment, and collaborative attitude. The efficiency of group approach is a function of many behavioral factors, which may be expressed as (Rajagopal and Rajagopal 2006):

$$p = f\,(m, a, g)$$

Where, p denotes the degree of performance, m represents motivation, a exhibits abilities of the individuals associated with the team, and g is expressed as realization of goals. The team may not function effectively if any of the mentioned factors or associated variables thereof are incoherent. The reward and punishment issues in a team emerge as a post-process synergy of all associated variables and are largely governed by the factors like common feeling, motivation, commitment, and collaborative attitude (Rajagopal 2006). Hence, teams are collections of people who must rely upon group collaboration if each member is to experience the optimum success and goal achievement. Changing technology and markets have stimulated the team approach in multinational companies for performing the organizational tasks. Moreover, the complexity of the society and human needs prompted team work as a significant tool in managing the corporate tasks (Dyer 1987). Team management is employed largely in the organizations where activities are less repetitive and predictable. Such an approach demands effective liaison, appropriate delegation of powers, judicious allocations of roles of team members, sharing of information, and accuracy in evaluation of team performance (Harris and Moran 1999).

Team control has emerged as a behavioral control mechanism. The sales engineers become a part of a quasi-firm arrangement, along with the client's engineers and managers, who supervise their work. Management efforts to ensure detailed documentation emerge as a second control mechanism (Darr 2003). Industrial organizations largely implement direct management control and influence the activities of employees leading toward improving their efficiency. The extent monitoring of sales managers, directing, evaluating, and rewarding activities in an organization intends to guide the sales team behavior through team control processes to achieve favorable results to the organization and the employees (Anderson and Oliver 1987). Team control in a sales organization is, thus, recognized as an important performance indicator of the task performed by the sales people. The innovation teams should be constituted with autonomy and enough scope for brainstorming on various task-related issues in the project. Constitution of teams should include the following attributes:

Warming: Educating the team members about the project and respective tasks of the members. Effective warming-up sessions would encourage the member of the project team to conceive the goals, objectives, tasks, and modalities of the innovation project.

Forming: Members exhibiting similar interests in the project and demonstrating the capability and competence in conducting tasks in the innovation projects should be pooled in a company to form an efficient project team. Attract like-minded people to get into the task and project management process.

Storming: It is a healthy practice to allow the members of the team to use their space in the team for loud thinking, discussions, debate over the issues, and present their point of view on managing the various tasks to be performed in the innovation projects.

Norming: Though brainstorming exercises result in arriving at common approaches, solutions to the problems, and taking preventive measures, there is a need to determine the rules and standards for open discussions on the innovation projects activities. This would streamline the participation of members within the team and keep them on track for carrying out the tasks in the project.

Performing: Teams constituted with the aforementioned attributes should be given autonomy or flexibility in decision making to conduct various tasks and enhance the performance of the project. However, the performance of teams should be monitored and evaluated on task-by-task basis to fix any advertence in the project operations process.

The SMART variables may be considered to administer sales teams which include: strategy orientation, measurability, approach, reality, and time frame. The strategy orientation would drive the brainstorming discussion to result orientation, and the measurability would count on the success of the deliberations (Rajagopal 2006). Teams, which need to work within an organization and across-functional activities such as sales, marketing, purchasing, personnel, and finance, find that team working fosters as collaborative tool rather than a competitive approach. It is important that terms of reference of teams must be capable of doing the job for which they have been selected, and this clearly implies that the membership should include people who are able to contribute toward the completion of task (McGreevy 2006). Every team should choose its leader and work in a collaborative pattern rather than a hierarchical structure. The team leadership should allow the members space for expressions, reviews, and suggestions during performing the project tasks. The company should offer task and project-specific training to the team members in delivering their services efficiently during the project period.

A new project is usually initiated with a kick-off meeting whether in a start-up enterprise or at a multinational company sponsoring the innovation project with SUEs. Accordingly, the purpose of the project, roles and responsibilities, and fitness of the project within the overall goals of the organization are explained among the project teams. This technique can be used in all types of teams. However, in a matrix project team, the kick-off meetings will be specific to the tasks and contextual to the deliverables within the cost and time frame. It is essential to establish the ground rules collaboratively in a team that will operate, which will provide the team with clarity and will ease communication over issues such as boundaries, responsibilities, and team member behavior. Functional teams already have this established through the use of departmental policies and procedures. However, for newly formed matrix project teams that do not have rules of operation established as part of their formal organization structure, team agreements are a necessary aspect of building an effective team.

References

Alden, D.L., J.B. Steenkamp, and R. Batra. 1999. "Brand Positioning Through Advertising in Asia, North America, and Europe: The Role of Global Consumer Culture." *Journal of Marketing* 63, no. 1, pp. 75–87.

Alden, D.L., J.B. Steenkamp, and R. Batra. 2006. "Consumer Attitudes Toward Marketplace Globalization: Structure, Antecedents and Consequences." *International Journal of Research in Marketing* 23, no. 3, pp. 227–39.

Anderson, E., and R.L. Oliver. 1987. "Perspectives on Behavior-Based Versus Outcome-Based Sales Team Control Systems." *Journal of Marketing* 51, no. 4, pp. 76–88.

Bartlett, C.A., and S. Ghoshal. 2002. "Building Competitive Advantage Through People." *MIT Sloan Management Review* 43, no. 2, pp. 35–42.

Bettencourt, L.A., and S.L. Bettencourt. 2011. "Innovating on the Cheap." *Harvard Business Review* 89, no. 6, pp. 88–94.

Bhide, A.V. 1994. "How Entrepreneurs Craft Strategies That Work." *Harvard Business Review* 72, no. 2, pp. 150–61.

Blank, S.G. 2013. "Why the Lean Start-Up Changes Everything." *Harvard Business Review* 91, no. 5, pp. 63–72.

Bremmer, I. 2014. "New Rules of Globalization." *Harvard Business Review* 92, no. 1, pp. 103–7.

Cohn, J., J. Katzenbach, and G. Vlak. 2008. "Finding and Grooming Breakthrough Innovators." *Harvard Business Review* 86, no. 12, pp. 62–68.

Collies, D.J. March 2016. "Lean Strategy." *Harvard Business Review*, pp. 62–68.

Cooper, R., and B. Maskell. 2008. "How to Manage Through Worse-Before-Better." *MIT Sloan Management Review* 49, no. 4, pp. 58–65.

Darr, A. 2003. "Control and Autonomy Among Knowledge Workers in Sales: An Employee Perspective." *Employee Relations* 25, no. 1, pp. 31–41.

deTreville, S., and L. Trigeorgis. 2010. "It May Be Cheaper to Manufacture at Home." *Harvard Business Review* 88, no. 10, pp. 84–87.

Dyer, W. 1987. *Team Building*, 20–23. Reading, MA: Addison-Wesley.

Eisenhardt, K.M., and D.N. Sull. 2001. "Strategy as Simple Rules." *Harvard Business Review* 79, no. 1, pp. 107–16.

Fernandez-Araoz, C., S. Iqbal, and J. Ritter. 2015. "Leadership Lessons from Great Family Businesses." *Harvard Business Review* 93, no. 4, pp. 82–88.

Garvin, D.A., and L.C. Levesque. 2006. "Meeting the Challenge of Corporate Entrepreneurship." *Harvard Business Review* 84, no. 10, pp. 102–12.

Ger, G., and R.W. Belk. 1996. "Cross-Cultural Differences in Materialism." *Journal of Economic Psychology* 17, no. 1, pp. 55–77.

Govindarajan, V., and R. Ramamurti. 2013. "Delivering World-Class Health Care, Affordably." *Harvard Business Review* 91, no. 11, pp. 117–22.

Hamel, G., and G. Getz. 2004. "Funding Growth in an Age of Austerity." *Harvard Business Review* 82, no. 7, pp. 76–84.

Hansen, G.E. 2002. *The Culture of Strangers—Globalization, Localization and the Phenomenon of Exchange.* New York: University Press of America.

Harris, P.R., and R.T. Moran. 1999. *Managing Cultural Difference-Leadership Strategies for a New World of Business,* 106–273. Huston, TX: Gulf Publishing Company.

Hills, G., D. Hansen, and C. Hultman. 2005. "A Value Creation View of Opportunity Recognition Processes." *International Journal of Entrepreneurship and Small Business* 2, no. 4, pp. 404–17.

Hultman, C.M., and G.E. Hills. 2011. "Influence from Entrepreneurship in Marketing Theory." *Journal of Research in Marketing and Entrepreneurship* 13, no. 2, pp. 120–25.

Jha, S.K., I. Parulkar, R. Krishnan, and C. Dhanaraj. 2016. "Developing New Products in Emerging Markets." *MIT Sloan Management Review* 57, no. 3, pp. 55–62.

Keidel, R.W. 2013. "Strategy Made Simple: Think in Threes." *Business Horizons* 56, no. 1, pp. 105–11.

Kelley, D. 2011. "Sustainable Corporate Entrepreneurship: Evolving and Connecting with the Organization." *Business Horizons* 54, no. 1, pp. 73–83.

Kogut, B. 1999. "What Makes a Company Global." *Harvard Business Review* 77, no. 1, pp. 165–70.

Kotabe, M., and K. Helsen. 2010. *Global Marketing Management.* 5th ed. Hoboken, NJ: John Wiley & Sons.

Lapre, M.A., and L.N. van Wassenhove. 2002. "Learning Across Lines: The Secret to More Efficient Factories." *Harvard Business Review* 80, no. 10, pp. 107–11.

Levitt, T. 1983. "Globalization of Markets." *Harvard Business Review* 61, no. 3, pp. 92–102.

Liu, W., B.D. Guillet, Q. Xiao, and R. Law. 2014. "Globalization or Localization of Consumer Preferences: The Case of Hotel Room Booking." *Tourism Management* 41, no. 2, pp. 148–57.

May, M.E. April 1, 2012. "Observe First, Design Second: Taming the Traps of Traditional Thinking." Working Paper, Ontario: Rotman School of Management.

McGreevy, M. 2006. "Team Working: How are Teams Chosen and Developed?" *Industrial and Commercial Training* 38, no. 7, pp. 365–70.

Miller, D., and I. le Breton-Miller. 2015. *What Every Small Business Can Learn from Great Family Firms: The 4C Advantage.* Cambridge, MA: Harvard Business Publishing.

Nayar, V. 2010. *Employees First, Customers Second: Turning Conventional Management Upside Down.* Boston, MA: Harvard Business School Press.

Ofek, E. 2013. *An Entrepreneur's New Product Development Journey.* Cambridge. MA: Harvard Business School Press.

Prahalad, C.K., and K. Lieberthal. 2003. "End of Corporate Imperialism." *Harvard Business Review* 76, no. 4, pp. 68–79.

Rajagopal. 2006. "Innovation and Business Growth through Corporate Venturing in Latin America: Analysis of Strategic Fit." *Management Decision* 44, no. 5, pp. 703–18.

Rajagopal, and A. Rajagopal. 2006. "Trust and Cross-Cultural Dissimilarities in Corporate Environment." *Team Performance Management* 12, nos. 7–8, pp. 237–52.

Rigby, D.K., and C. Zook. 2002. "Open Market Innovation." *Harvard Business Review* 80, no. 10, pp. 80–89.

Ritzer, G. 2007. *The Globalization of Nothing 2.* Thousand Oaks, CA: Pine Porge Press.

Robertson, R. 1987. "Globalization and Societal Modernization: A Note on Japan and Japanese Religion." *Sociological Analysis* 47, pp. 35–43.

Robertson, R. 1995. "Glocalization: Time-Space and Homogeneity-Heterogeneity." In *Global Modernities,* eds. M. Featherstone, S. Lash, and R. Robertson. London: Sage.

Saikat, B., and A. Aneja. 2014. *ONergy: Developing a Social Entrepreneurship Start-up Brand.* Ontario, Canada: Ivey Publishing, Richard Ivey School of Business.

Sarasvathy, S. 2001. "Causation and Effectuation: Toward a Theoretical from Economic Inevitability to Entrepreneurial Contingency." *Academy of Management Review* 26, no. 2, pp. 243–63.

Schweer, M., D. Assimakopoulos, R. Cross, and R.J. Thomas. 2012. "Building a Well-Networked Organization." *MIT Sloan Management Review* 53, no. 2, p. 35.

Steenkamp, J.B., and M.G. De Jong. 2010. "A Global Investigation into the Constellation of Consumer Attitudes Toward Global and Local Products." *Journal of Marketing* 74, no. 6, pp. 18–40.

Sull, D.N. 2004. "Disciplined Entrepreneurship." *MIT Sloan Management Review* 46, no. 1, pp. 71–78.

Tiffin, S., and M. Carmona. 2004. *Fundacion Chile: Creating Innovative Enterprises.* Cambridge, MA: Harvard Business School Press.

Ulwick, A.W. 2002. "Turn Customer Input to Innovation." *Harvard Business Review* 80, no. 1, pp. 91–97.

Webb, J.W., D.J. Ketchen, Jr., and R.D. Ireland. 2010. "Strategic Entrepreneurship Within Family-Controlled Firms: Opportunities and Challenges." *Journal of Family Business Strategy* 1, no. 2, pp. 67–77.

Wheeler, M.A. April 1, 2004. "Turn Chaos to Your Advantage." *Negotiation* 7, no. 4, pp. 3–5.

Wolpert, J.D. 2002. "Breaking Out of the Innovation Box." *Harvard Business Review* 80, no. 8, pp. 77–84.

Wood, I.J., and S. Grosvenor. 2003. "Chocolate in China: The Cadbury Experience." *Australian Geographer* 28, no. 2, pp. 173–84.

Woodward, H.N. 1976. "Management Strategies for Small Companies." *Harvard Business Review* 54, no. 1, pp. 113–21.

Yu, Y.C., W.H. Byun, and T.J. Lee. 2013. "Critical Issues of Globalization in the International Hotel Industry." *Current Issues in Tourism* 17, no. 2, pp. 114–18.

Zahra, S.A., and S. Nambisan. 2012. "Entrepreneurship and Strategic Thinking in Business Ecosystems." *Business Horizons* 55, no. 3, pp. 219–29.

Zou, S., and S.T. Cavusgil. 2002. "The GMS: A Brand Conceptualization of Global Marketing Strategy and its Effect on Firm Performance." *Journal of Marketing* 66, no. 4, pp. 40–56.

CHAPTER 4

Project Environment

Overview

A company must excel in two seemingly parallel ways to become a leader in global markets with innovative product differentiations. First, the company should constantly build and refresh its market segments with innovative and differentiated products, so that it grows with the critical capabilities needed to stay ahead. Second, they should proceed systematically in planning and implementing business projects, integrating the internal and external factors to work together in an ever-changing competitive environment. Most companies have recognized that cross-functional process of implementing business projects builds functional excellence. This chapter addresses the factors of internal and external environment that drive the project implementation process in different business situations. In continuation to the discussion on project environmental factors, this chapter also discusses project matrix and project lifecycle. Innovative business projects are the juncture where functional groups work together within the organization's integrated abilities. Resource planning, financial evaluations, and managerial training to carry on the projects, which strengthen the project relationship among functions, have been discussed in this chapter.

Project Administration

Innovation business projects are largely influenced by the project environment built over various internal and external factors, and project lifecycle. The internal environment of an innovation project is architected by the organizational culture, resources, and risk management abilities, while the external environment is governed by market and collaborative moves on managing innovative projects. Innovation-led business projects can operate successfully, when project teams stay streamlined with the organizational culture and are empowered for decision making, exercising autonomy for project operations. Such supremacy to the innovation project teams would help them resolve many problems during the project management process. Commitment of employees and members of the project team is very closely allied with empowerment. The organizational culture generally resists any changes in the project goals, tasks, and techniques designed to accelerate the project implementation process, if thrusted on the project team either abruptly or in a transparent transitional manner. The innovative projects are largely implemented in a controlled environment and are sensitive to the internal environment of the organization. The project teams develop confrontation if the top-down decision flow dominates the project task management environment by stipulating the messages like "carry on your task, the way we tell you." Under such circumstances, members of the project teams feel little commitment, express change proneness, and feel less empowered in the organization (Argyris 1998).

Project management administration, techniques, team attributes, and organizational culture play key roles in building the project environment in a company. The project environment requisites in a company are often complex in reference to product development, making efficient use of resources, and stimulating cross-functional tasks and communication. The significance of innovative business projects today is not only limited to manufacturing firms, but has also made a significant dent in judiciary by way of digitization of proceedings, enterprise resource planning, health care sector companies, and local governments as an indispensable part of their operations. Such widespread acceptance of innovation in manufacturing and services industries has led to various challenges in managing innovation projects. However, such manifold growth of innovation project is not out of bounds of failures and outright disasters. Among various factors that contribute toward the failure of an innovation project include ignoring its environment, working in an unacceptable organizational culture, pushing a new technology to market immaturely, developing high expectations on the performance of team members, considering low priority on the project's fallback options, and fixing loose accountability of project managers. The project environment demands to stay abreast with the project management performance management techniques by conducting feasibility studies, developing macro perspective of team management, and building strong leadership with strategic orientation and goal-oriented project planning (Pinto and Kharbanda 1996).

Internal and External Fit

As the market competition is growing continuously in the global marketplace, innovation has become a survival instinct for companies, and they tend to invest perennially on the innovation and new product development projects to maintain competitive differentiation. In this process of innovation initiatives, the organizations often undergo many changes in workplace environment, cross-cultural conflicts, and decision-making issues due to the formation of new project teams and working with collaborative ventures. Hence, it is difficult for most companies to maintain the internal fit of innovation project teams with the organization, and they often suffer from conflicts in task management in reference to taking decision, monitoring the performance, and balancing the time and cost performance during the project. The internal environment of the project encompasses the following factors:

- Team culture
- Working relationships
- Open communications
- An environment of trust
- Willingness to take risks
- Recognition of efforts and achievements

Managing innovation projects is a not just driven through the power of leaders, but it needs a homogeneous team to carry out multilevel tasks. The project leaders should follow good recruitment practices for inducting members of the project teams, set achievable expectations, constantly monitor performance feedback, manage conflict, and determine critical success factors for building an efficient innovation project team. While companies recognize the critical value of a team to work on innovation projects, the importance of cultivating a cooperative mindset should be considered as a prime attribute to inculcate into the project teams (Gratton 2007). The working relationship at various hierarchical levels in the organization beyond the teams should be healthy to manage with bottom-up approach that allows listening, analyzing, and acting on the voices of the team members. Top-down decision approach for the working relationship is also considered to be fine, provided the innovation project teams are not clutched with bureaucratic administration. In developing a seemly project environment, flexibility in working relationships needs to be considered. Project teams often function in a matrix format, staffed by members taken from diverse functional teams in order to achieve the project goal. When the project manager exercises a high degree of authority, the team is known as a strong matrix, whereas the team is identified as a weak matrix when functional managers have stronger authority over the project leader. Some companies also believe in constituting the functional teams that are less autocratic. The attributes of functional and autonomous teams in managing innovative business projects are exhibited in Table 4.1.

A company periodically needs to evaluate its organizational environment, regardless of the competitive landscape of the company in the industry. Even if the external environment is not changing in ways that demand a response, companies need to maintain the internal environment that probably encourages the employees to work on innovation projects. The human dynamics within an organization are constantly shifting. The most growing challenge in an organization is managing change for assuring the internal fit. Over time, informal networks

Table 4.1 Attributes of functional and autonomous teams

Functional teams	Autonomous teams
• Typically use marketing and sales projects • Identical spread of work groups • Team members may be assigned to the project either full time or part time • The project manager does not have complete authority over the project team • Updated to functional managers	• More than one business projects • Company works on multiple projects at any given time, usually high dollar value and long-term projects • One project team for one project • Each project is operated like a minicompany • There is little opportunity for members of different project teams to share knowledge or technical expertise

within the teams mirror the formal structure, which triggers the advantages of restructuring human resources to start a bottom-up democratic environment to carry out the innovation projects, making the organization more creative. Such internal fit in an organization collectively stifle innovation and adaptability processes and prepare the employees for the change management for designing, developing, and implementing the innovative business projects without personal or organizational conflicts (Vermeulen, Puranam, and Gulati 2010). The internal fit in an organization can be achieved by adhering to the following requirements:

- Conveying clear goals and objectives to the employees
- Transparency in the management process
- Flow of communication within the organization with disruption in contents
- Clear accountability of employees and project team
- Systematic monitoring and evaluation
- Follow a single reporting channel for measuring performance than allowing multiple authorities to supervise the performance of an employee
- Following the core of ethics within the organizational policy
- Allowing interpersonal communication with in the organization
- Honoring the voice of employees on innovation, management, and operational processes
- Embedding team culture and cooperation in managing tasks than creating the competitive environment by setting targets against the peers
- Maintaining integrity and confidentiality of matters within employees to protect the competitiveness of the organization
- Develop cooperation and trust in the organizational culture

There are four factors that make higher impact on the employee of an organization, including intangible job context, employee development and skill utilization, remuneration packages and workplace, culture and rewards (Qu, Ryan, and Chu 2001). Work ethics play a major role in developing organizational learning and integrating the learning process with work culture to strategically fit into the organizational design and structure. Although improved compliance procedures can help limit this risk, successful efforts must extend beyond compliance to build a culture of organizational integrity. Recent changes in regulatory requirements in financial institutions and more guidelines on monitoring and performance evaluation demand an integrated approach to cultural awareness through the four organizational practices of controls, clearly defined principles and purpose, core values, and ethics. Inevitably, the most difficult of these is building a culture of high ethical standards that are reflected in day-to-day practice (Kayes, Stirling, and Nielsen 2007).

Organizational learning is a continuous process, and it involves employees at all levels of management in sharing knowledge and innovative insights, which supports the business growth of the firm. The learning process is generally embedded in the organizational culture that drives employees to invest resources in creative thinking. The organizational culture comprising the task, thrust, time, target, and territory of work stimulates the learning process. Alike diffusing knowledge with the employees, often organizations learn innovative ideas by committing trials and errors within the organization. Another behavioral dimension that appears to be critical in determining the employer and employee relationship is the opportunity of unlearning knowledge and skills of the employees. Often firms succeed in convincing highly talented candidates to accept lower positions, assuring that they will be promoted to the position that has a close match with their qualification and experience, but employees under such situations succumb to frustration as they do not find an appropriate platform to share their knowledge and implement skills.

Driving forced internal fit in an organization through managerial control would lead employees of the firm to develop resistance and defeat the objective of the firm to commonly acquire contemporary skills, design thinking, and develop innovative strategies. It may be appropriate for the emerging firms to consider a review of integrated learning designs for improving the unit effectiveness. Learning environment in an enterprise is largely governed by the organizational culture, which is affected directly and indirectly by the employee relationship and their behavioral performance (Rajagopal and Rajagopal 2008). The level of diffusion of knowledge in the organization largely depends on the learning design comprising individual, peer, and subject-oriented or interdisciplinary patterns. Learning and application of knowledge in an organization is often motivated by reward systems orchestrated to generate the desired synergy in reference to its contents and use value. In a global marketplace, which is perpetually changing, the learning organizations must support the idea that diffusion and adaptation of innovative ideas, managerial know-how, and business strategy are continuous processes. However, a number of traditional organizations tend to discourage such knowledge process by limiting the financial and human resources. Thus, emerging enterprises should rethink on choosing the most appropriate learning design for the organization in reference to managing information acquisition and diffusion processes, and break the conventional knowledge barriers in organizational learning. There are various knowledge-based perspectives that affect the internal fit of the employees in a company toward innovations and diffusion, discussed as follows:

- Inadequate information on innovation, research and development, and design
- Lack of qualified personnel within the enterprise or in the labor market
- Lack of information on technology and markets
- Deficiencies in the availability of external services
- Difficulty in finding co-operation partners for innovative products, process development, and strategic business alliances
- Organizational rigidities within the enterprise like attitude of personnel or managers toward change and managerial structure of enterprise
- Inability to devote staff to innovation activity due to production requirements

A major setback in achieving the internal fit in a company is the cry over random budgetary allocation for the projects and tasks that demoralize the employee expectations with the high-value projects involving time-bound innovation and commercialization. When teams head up a big innovation project, they need to uphold the motivation of their team members and avoid either squandering or limiting the use of available capital. It is important to create and manage the innovative project complying to the mission and implement a truly energizing work environment that establishes a right internal fit for the teams to work. The only way to get the best internal fit for innovation project teams is acceptable work environment, admissible autonomy, availability of resources, output-oriented monitoring, fair evaluation, great design, and innovative features that match with the business goals of the company to achieve the desired performance. Hence, rolling back to the first step to get the best internal fit, it is necessary to assemble the right team, and then staying involved, responding to hard questions about organizational culture and workplace environment. Innovation-led organizations should articulate a vision for future work space and drive the search for ways to realize this vision matches the new innovative business projects with the market behavior (Thurm 2005).

Knowledge management involves many procedures and techniques used to get the most from an organization's explicit and tacit know-how. Sharing knowledge without personal bias among peers or employees within the organization is the most important critical success factor of all knowledge management strategies. Effective knowledge sharing practices allow individuals to reuse and regenerate knowledge at the individual and organizational level (Chaudhry 2005). However, most enterprises observe individual and organizational barriers in knowledge sharing that include internal resistance, trust, motivation, and inadequate awareness. Learning organizations require a change in focus from a technology-driven approach to a people-driven approach to improve knowledge management. With the evolution of technology, the paradigm of knowledge management is shifting from a conventional approach to an analytical approach as a conversational medium by combining formal and informal knowledge within a social context (Hong, Suh, and Koo 2011).

To be a leader in global innovation, a company must excel in two seemingly contradictory ways. Firstly, it must constantly build and refresh its individual areas of expertise from the point of commercialization of innovation, so that it attains the critical capabilities needed to stay ahead, and secondly, it must be a perfect internal fit within various disciplines and project teams to work together to meet the required output for a competitive marketplace. Most companies have reorganized themselves by cross-functional processes, have already discovered the ways who integrate various disciplines and still maintain the core functional excellence. However, innovative projects often reach the critical juncture where functional groups have to make compromise with the organization's integrative abilities that affect the quality of output and commercialization process to build the brands of new innovative products in the market. The internal fit in an innovation organization is used as a tool for strengthening the relationship among functions and develop expertise in the specific field to build the market leadership and gain competitiveness in the marketplace (Leonard-Barton et al. 1994).

External Fit

Forward linkages to innovative business projects comprising technology alliances, supply chain, marketing, branding, services management, and customer relations that are managed by the entities outside the principal organization constitute the external fit. Outsourcing of task to be supplemented for carrying out the tasks in an innovation project has emerged as most cost-effective and functionally efficient trend among the companies today. The relationship with outsourced agencies and alliances with other companies appear to be the major challenges for the innovation companies. The start-up enterprises (SUEs) are largely involved in sprouting new ideas and bringing out the prototypes with testing in the niche markets, attracting sponsors for global commercialization. Hence, most large companies operating in the regional or global markets tend to outsource the innovation and new product development process to the SUEs. For instance, VanceInfo and Microsoft had been engaged in a long-term client or vendor relationship since 1997, and the project had been the result of this long-term partnership arrangement. The project was deemed quite successful and innovative as it provided an opportunity to determine how collaborative innovation could work between two remote and culturally different supply chain partners (Abbott, Zheng, and Du 2013).

Innovation and enterprise integration are two compelling sources of growth in a dynamic competitive marketplace. The ability to coordinate across organizational boundaries largely appears as a critical factor in determining the speed and lifecycle of a market-driven innovation. Innovations need to be integrated into the larger operations of the corporation at sufficient level of scale to show a prolific impact on business and sustainability in the marketplace. Many large businesses spend resources on innovations, but fail to capitalize on them. However, some organizations use innovations to optimize local operations than integrating them to create consumer value and corporate image. Large organizations spread the innovation tasks among two groups comprising innovation facilities group (IFG) and an innovation assimilation group. The IFG members provide organizational support on the techniques to carry out innovations and applications for the new technology. Firms also engage the IFG to explore new developments in the marketplace on the concept, prototypes, or breakthrough of the innovation and impart expert services for in-house initiatives to nurture the innovation within the organization. The innovation assimilation group acts as policy support unit to drive innovation to market. The members of this team provide resources to launch innovation, and integrate operations into the business model of the firm. Firms need the aforementioned support teams to diffuse innovation and make it more (Cash, Earl, and Morison 2008).

Companies outsourcing the innovation process need to develop a conducive work environment by synchronizing the external fit with the outsources organizations like SUEs through the following steps:

- Defining mutually fit objectives
- Collaborating in management of resources and inputs required for the innovation projects
- Co-creating innovation infrastructure
- Revising the backward linkages and developing internal fit within the organization to coordinate with the outsourced enterprises
- Executing innovation process in a task-by-task manner with the outsourced enterprise
- Monitoring progress categorically
- Monitoring, evaluation, and administering checks and balances on innovation project

- Developing a business plan and working with the market players supporting the commercialization of innovation
- Launching the innovated product, offering customer services, and delivering value to stakeholders.

Firms must ensure that all innovations should encompass attributes of four As comprising awareness, acceptability, availability, and affordability to diffuse innovation in the overall market. The attributes of internal and external fit within and outside organization for planning and implementation of innovation projects is exhibited in Figure 4.1.

The ease of internal and external fitness for carrying out innovation projects largely depends on the organizational design and decision systems such as vertical (top-down) or horizontal (team or bottom-up), as illustrated in the Figure 4.1. The information and business analytics helps companies to make appropriate decisions toward achieving internal and external fit required for not only managing the innovation projects efficiently, but also to plan commercialization of new products by developing forward linkages with the suppliers, retailers, service providers, and customer relations management. Companies managing innovations as

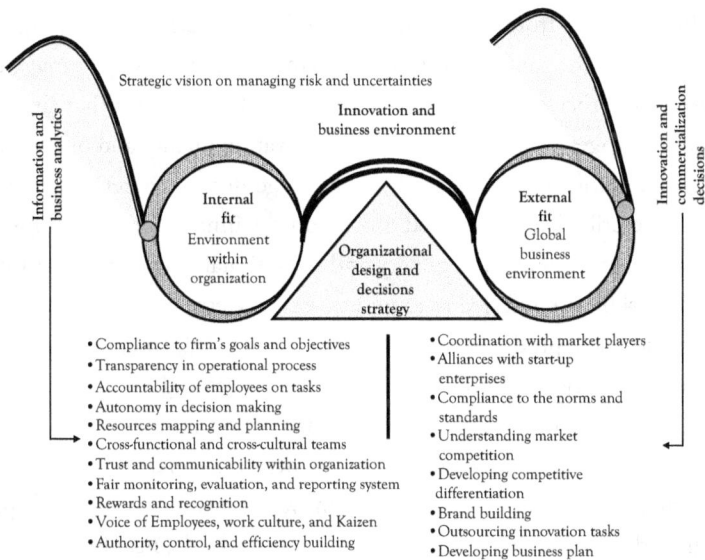

Figure 4.1 Analyzing organizational environment for managing external and internal fit

a continuous process to establish competitiveness and brand loyalty of new products should develop strategic vision also to counter the risk and uncertainties in the product development as well as in the commercialization processes. Unforeseen uncertainty and chaos in the innovation companies are common, and companies need to strike a balance between planning and continuous learning. Companies must learn to ascertain what kind of uncertainty is likely to dominate a project by following the most suitable mix of project tools and techniques to work with the innovation projects (de Meyer, Loch, and Pich 2002). The factors influencing the external fit of a company include the following attributes:

- Market demand
- Capabilities and competencies of innovation sponsors
- Technological advancement
- Government norms and standard
- Political, economic, social, technological, and legal factors
- Understanding consumers and consumerism

The innovation assimilation group should help in developing the task-map for the innovation team and integrate the process map by identifying the goal from the perspectives of consumers. By mapping out every step of the innovation task, companies can effectively manage the innovation process (Bettencourt and Ulwick 2008). A firm that simultaneously engages a high degree of both innovation quality and operational efficiency gains higher competitive advantage in the market in reference to the prescribed and perceived quality on the innovation. Few firms are able to balance innovation quality and operational efficiency. Such management skills are referred as ambidextrous strategy, which differentiates firms and their products from the competing products and help them enjoy temporary monopoly in the market (Sarkees and Hulland 2008).

Unless an enterprise generates information on business environment and diffuses it efficiently throughout its organizational network among the employees and members of the innovation team, it could well play with market uncertainties and secure the market for the near future. Many companies rely on an information technology and knowledge management infrastructure with the social system in which people operate the sociocommercial ecology of innovative products of a company. Socio-commercial ecology drives people's expectations, defines consumption approaches, guides perceptions on innovations, demand pricing and promotion strategies from the company, identifies the right consumer segments that will fit in the commercialization of innovations, and determines consumer interactions on the new innovative products through various networks. Through effective management of knowledge, Nucor developed and constantly upgraded its main strategic and proprietary competencies: plant construction and start-up know-how, manufacturing process expertise, and the ability to adopt breakthrough technologies earlier than competitors. Nucor's sociocommercial ecology also allowed, among other things, excellence in the tasks associated with sharing and mobilizing knowledge by identifying opportunities to share knowledge, building effective and efficient transmission channels, and convincing individuals to accept and use the innovation and change-driven products (Gupta and Govindarajan 2000).

Transfer of Innovation and Technology

Most innovative products that are launched in the market soon attract competition and face the challenge of substitution, while some products compete with low-end and disruptive technology products. In both situations, innovative products struggle for their existence in the market and attempt to fit into the consumer perceptions positively. Yet most organizations naturally resist change and pull out from investing in brand building and communication to support the survival of innovative products. Most resourceful companies hold change to innovate and succeed by meticulously distinguishing between their core and context activities and integrating the right innovation model to their business strategy.

Transforming markets for adapting product and services innovations is a big challenge for most companies engaged in doing business in consumer products. Innovative products need to be transformed to the perceived suitability of consumers for optimal use by way of total customization. Most innovative products have the limitation for 360° transformations due to the standardized functionality and built-in structural restrictions. Driving change in the marketplace demand and consumer behavior has traditionally come through top-down initiatives such as corporate endorsements toward manufacturing design, quality, technology, and innovation for new products experts and developing marketing best practices to inculcate perceived changes in consumer behavior. Critical innovations in consumer products like light emitting diode (LED) screens and lighting devices transformed consumer behavior and market demand to get more value at less price. Transforming buying behavior for such innovations is relatively easy than educating consumers toward the use of innovation in educational products and services. But within every organization, there are a few product innovations that encounter unique marketing problems that seem impossible to solve. Although these change-agent products in a company roll out in the market with effective communication tools to drive awareness, attractiveness, trial, availability, and repeat buying stimulus, they often fail to gain consumer confidence in usability and so fail to generate the desired response in the market. Companies can develop innovation launch and transformation to consumer need strategies considering the following attributes:

- Co-create community orientation and engage the process of self-appraisal of innovative products and services in terms of competitive benefits and value for money
- Reframe innovation through facts and prepare for innovation transformation according to the customer needs and market demand
- Entail marketing of innovative products in the existing channel network and allow direct marketing to create customer value
- Make innovation safe to learn among consumers and market players by creating an environment that builds constructive opinions
- Grow communication grapevine through the digital networks and physical community infrastructure on the innovations and competitive advantages
- Make the innovations as problem solver and drive it in the market as a key to the community satisfaction

- Leverage social evidences for the innovation considering its applications to the larger community-led consumer awareness like ecofriendly detergents that minimize cesspool and soil pollution
- Build immunity to innovations in the market against disruptions and misevaluations that could build low trust and commitment among the consumers and market players

Companies should ensure that throughout following the aforementioned steps, they must adopt a facilitator's role without overpowering the consumers or raising conflicts with the competitors. Such corporate attitude may cause damage to the brand image of the company. The customer-centric innovation transformation methodology can help solve even the most extreme dilemmas on innovation acceptability in the market and its socialization for sustained growth (Pascale and Sternin 2005). Companies that organize their innovation transformation efforts in systematic, well-managed ways are those whose efforts will be rewarded in terms of high rate of acceptance among consumers, distribution harmony, and retailing diligence. The systematic model of innovation management of companies should link to strategy, problem solving, and cultural change, and tailored to the needs consumers.

Cultivating continual innovation and creating new business models have become essential success parameters for any business. Vertical and horizontal integrations are imperative to the success of a corporation, resulting in models that provide tremendous business opportunities. This approach also brings great execution challenges. In addition to creating innovation through internal research and development, two significant areas where enterprises constantly strive to create innovative capabilities are mergers and acquisitions and partner strategies. Innovation and new business models can be successfully enabled through connecting specific products and solutions. A robust network foundation is essential for building higher level infrastructure services. This foundation includes intelligent network capabilities at the different network locations, including branch offices and campuses, external connectivity, and home and partner environments. A converged network infrastructure can result in major savings when collaboration and video are enabled along with the right productivity solutions, for instance, through the use of unified communications and collaboration technologies, immersive video, and video phones. A key technical requirement to scale business models is faster service provisioning. Through the use of a private cloud and intelligent automation solutions, corporations can reduce the time taken to provision a new service. Embracing virtual desktop technologies can also result in considerable advantages.

Innovation is broadly considered as an intellectual accomplishment at the grassroots of humanity, but commercializing it is a business skill compounded with capabilities, competencies, and resources of the organizations. Thus, most business innovations are either developed by entrepreneurs or small and medium enterprises, but they lead to mergers or acquisition with a larger business organization to gain enough resources to grow in the marketplace. Most of the innovations driving potential businesses are acquired by the large companies and carried forward to develop commercially and position them sustainably in the marketplace. For example, in small information technology companies, young software developers have worked on developing the interactive shopper software to support the consumers on selecting clothing and dresses that are suitable to their appearance and taste online. This software was later made available for personal computers, local area networks, Android phones, and many more devices. The virtual dressing room can be installed in any place that has electricity and broadband Internet access, and the developers hope to eventually see the unit installed in areas like train stations and airport terminals. The technology, called *tryvertising*, is already popular in Japan, where some of the early trials have taken place. The system works by using a Kinect sensor along with a 60-inch LCD display and an iPad. It is able to respond instantly to the user's movements as they try on the clothing, and the developers claim that the system can even provide a virtual experience of the clothing's texture. Once an item has been selected, the shopper can use a printed QR code to access the item at the online store and complete the purchase. Mergers and acquisitions for product and service innovations require a combination of solutions that work to seamlessly integrate the marketing-mix, and this process also brings challenges related to varied information and technology-related market environments. Most companies struggle with the process of integrating the physical and intellectual capital of a new acquisition into the parent environment.

Innovations of some small companies that emerge in a niche are able to radically change their entrenched ways of serving the large markets and claim leading transformation in the market. Even less common are companies that are able to anticipate a new set of requirements and mobilize the internal and external resources necessary to meet the innovation transformation process. Few companies make the transformation from their market-oriented business innovation model to a customer-centric innovation management model, which delivers the innovation to the consumers in a sustainable way with high level of satisfaction. Innovation transformation typically begins at the niche market, searching a way forward to create a new consumer segment to sustain by developing a temporary monopoly situation. This seeks the following clarifications for companies to manage the transformation of innovation of products and services from premium consumer segment to mass segment and finally down to the bottom of the pyramid:

- Is differentiating innovations by the consumer or market segment a prolific strategy?
- Do companies really need to develop differentiated marketing strategy to transform innovations and galvanize change?
- How could it be possible for the companies to adopt new ways of managing transformed innovation in view of the preferences of consumers under market pressure?

Most companies develop new dynamic capabilities deliberately to manage the innovation transformation and market management process. Companies that transform the innovations to the consumer preferences gain fundamental advantages over the competitors toward building marketing alliances of branding and distribution, creating experiential marketing challenging in business against conventionally operating competitors, and nurturing strategic changes in consumer behavior (Johnson, Yip, and Hensmans 2012).

Project Matrix

The innovation projects have to be monitored and evaluated, implemented based on various cross-sectional factors that directly or indirectly affect the project performance. These factors are largely common for innovation projects, but may vary for specific projects under external business environment factors. A project management model integrates the project matrix, which shows the cause and effect and the interrelationship among the key operational factors affecting the outcome of innovation projects. The project matrix should be constructed as a visual map of the task, time, cost, and outcome expectations during the phases of the innovation project. The project matrix is an integrating tool that provides a single design for organizing the goals, developing related tasks, and reviewing the diverse aspects of the innovation project:

- The work breakdown explaining the small tasks groups spread over the divided timeframe of the project for easy stage (phase)-gate (review) process,
- Preparing the documents of deliverables in reference to documents, drawings, listings, and so on
- The task management in reference to cost-time-risk triadic critical variables in an innovation project
- Developing the project charter by delineating the accountability of people to tasks, goals, objectives, deliverables, and the quantity and types of skills required to complete the project
- The project's engineering standards, design, and operational modalities and project methodology

The project matrix can be designed through the various project supporting software including Microsoft Project to delineate the effective coordination among people associated with innovation projects, managing the operations, reducing the complexity during the innovation process, and producing high-quality results. A sample of multiple-task matrix for innovation projects is illustrated in Table 4.2.

Companies engaged in managing innovation projects may structure the project matrix in reference to the basic project indicators during the

Table 4.2 Multitask matrix for innovation projects

	Mission goals objectives	Human resources	Capital cost interest and profit	Time-phasing and extensions	Technology-feasibility viability	Marketing sales demand risk	Market information and business analytics	Next-generation innovation and growth
Project prologue								
Project requirements								
Project design								
External specifications								
Project outcome								
Prototype testing								
Business plan and commercialization								
Monitoring and evaluation								

initiation phase and later expand it with the advanced project management elements. The matrix should begin with project prologue, which should specify the mission, goals, and objectives of the project, and various functional elements like time, cost, resources, market demand, and business environment supporting the innovation-led products or services, as exhibited in Table 4.2. The project matrix helps the managers and project teams to determine the project requirement and work on designing in considering the vital indicators as discussed earlier. The business plan for an innovation project outcome should be evaluated in the project matrix in reference to CTR (cost, time, and risk) factors and its marketability. The project team should prepare the matrix by mentioning specific goals of the project and develop documents for the project, considering the monitoring CTR subsystem. Accordingly, the information should be collected and placed in the corresponding columns and rows of the matrix to serve as a guiding tool throughout the project duration. The project matrix and project subsystems are clearly defined into the sets of deliverables through various phases in the projects and are attended methodically to complete the task. The project manager should develop the matrix, which lays out the tasks in terms of the phase-wise outputs. Upon evaluation of the output in each phase, the project staff is required to produce intermediate deliverables for internal review or for external delivery to the client on demand. The project planning matrix (PPM) shows both the logical structure of the project that links between the inputs or activities and the objectives to be achieved under predetermined assumptions and the attributes that are critical to quality. The PPM is useful in the project planning process by advising the planner to constantly check whether the project design is plausible and consistent, and facilitating the communication among all members of the teams on the why's and the how's of the project, allowing project monitoring based on common understanding (Gottfredson and Aspinall 2005). The matrix structure of the project management has several benefits in delivering the quality output in reference to the following attributes:

- Accountability
  - In a matrix organization, it is important to delineate the project management responsibilities and the functional management responsibilities.

- Power equilibrium
  - When implementing a matrix organizational structure, the operating guidelines should be established to assure proper balance of power between project managers and functional managers.
- Size of the teams
  - Project teams should be kept as small as possible throughout the project.

The innovation projects generally do not fail working on an innovation project through a well-set matrix base, but management needs to ensure implementing each scheduled task successfully. In managing an innovation project, strategy, structure, processes, rewards, and people all need to be aligned in a successful matrix implementation. There are many challenges in developing a right project matrix and implementing it within the project environment where accountability of project team members should be defined in reference to the following attributes:

- Rationale—Project managers need to assure that the team members understand the context of all elements of the matrix and develop their attitude and behavior toward working with the project and preparing the right deliverables.
- Cooperation—The project matrix is intended to improve cooperation among the cross-functional teams in managing the tasks, without encouraging bureaucracy, leading to slower decisions by involving too many.
- Control—It is recommended to have autonomy among teams and control standards for checks and balances on managing tasks. Centralization of controls can make the matrix slow and expensive that may lead to cost and time overrun. The project managers should build trust in distributed and diverse teams and to empower people to work with their tasks.

The project matrix not only has a significant impact within the technical domain, but it also serves as a guiding tool for the sponsors and project administrators outside the project domain. The two project matrix can have many variables in rows and columns in odd or even format depending on the nature of the innovation project. The effect and value of the rows and columns address the robust weight and measure of the variables associated with the respective tasks to be performed across the predetermined stages of management of innovation projects. This is a divide and conquer approach, and the benefit is a reduction of complexity in the given CTR framework. The goal is to define a set of columns to place the factors of governing systems like human resources, CTR, deliverables, marketing, and so on, that are relatively dependent of one another. The tasks can, thus, be conducted in continuum, and a project model can be set up with specific criteria of success. In this process, it is suggested to develop a pilot model for testing and then build a detailed deliverables-based project model. Matrix and hybrid structures in project management are being opted by most organizations that intend to engage in bringing innovations to the market continuously. The major attributes of the matrix and hybrid product structure include:

- Multiple projects are in progress at any given time
- Projects vary in size and complexity
- Hybrid structure—a mix of both the functional and autonomous project organizational structures
- Provides for effective utilization of company resources
  - Employee assignments—full project time
  - Career development and growth
  - Have a dual reporting relationship with a (temporary) project manager and a (permanent) functional manager
- Project manager is the intermediary between the company and the stakeholders
- Checks and balances and fast response upon problem identification

The hybrid structure of project management is a combination of both models of functional and autonomous project management teams. Such blended constitution of project teams would allow the companies to host multiple innovation projects of varying size and complexity with long-term engagement of employees. The hybrid project teams would be able to make optimum use of organizational resources—both human and capital resources—and maintain required checks and balances during the project execution process. However, the hybrid project teams will work with dual reporting system with the leader of the functional unit as well as the project leader.

Administrative complexities play a significant role in explaining new technology drive. Process simplification, zero defect products, cost and profit, and overall governance of new products development have many odds to be either eliminated or managed within the organizational system. Most managers exert in never having considered setting up business, thinking about the odds and complexities or think about them during the process and give up the innovation process. Such behavior is also significantly affected by the perception of administrative complexity (van Stel and Stunnenberg 2006). Firms that are engaged in rapid development of new products find the gap between diffusion and adoption. It is expensive for companies to manage the overpiled inventory of obsolete products unless they can be improved and reverted to the active demand. Expensive downtime for production-line changeovers, and merchandise languishing on retailers' shelves or in their showrooms also cause serious concerns to the firms engaged in developing new products. For service companies, though, complexity is much harder to spot and root out, largely due to the ease with which new products can be created and marketed (Gottfredson and Schwedel 2008).

Large organizations are complex by nature and face new business challenges, such as globalization, innovative technologies, and regulations over the period. Market uncertainties and competitive threats add layer upon layer of complexity to corporate structure and management. Technology marketing is complex, and most firms get trapped into the complexity grid; however, some get over the problems as they develop sustainability against uncertainties and work through the new challenges. The innovation marketing grid has several factors that pose conflicts and challenges to the innovation project management companies during different levels of the process. The complexity grid comprises 12 commonly observed points of conflicts, with independent effects of each point as well as their combined effect in a matrix form. The conflict points in the grid include ideation, resources management, process management, capabilities and competencies, technology marketing, growth and next-generation innovation and technology issues, involvement, organizational policies, operational efficiency, competitive decision, business environment, and organizational culture, all of which nurture the innovation and technology development projects in the firm. In the complexity grid ideation process and the extent of involvement of employees, consumers, and market players stage cognitive and organizational conflicts and challenges, while management of resources and organizational policies raise various challenging issues during different phases of innovation and technology development. Similarly, the process and operational efficiency commonly drive various issues of concern in reference to capabilities and competencies, and work culture of the organization. Firms face many conflicts during the innovation process on marketing of the technology-led products and the existing business environment. Moving the innovation and technology to next generation is also not an easy step-up as firms often get snared in the unwise competitive decisions in an effort to push the innovation and technology-led products in the marketplace (Rajagopal 2014).

Large firms have been the driving force behind the market economies in the developed countries. Traditional theories suggest that new products that are not consistent with the existing demand retard economic growth, whereas classical theories suggest that serving products to the existing market demand is safer than creating demand in the market to position the products. However, the global competition and changing consumer behavior on experimenting new products have raised new theoretical concepts on the relationship of launching new products with the market demand. Large firms are engaged in continuously developing new products and could benefit, in contrast to small firms, from economies of scale and scope. Many economists believed that larger firms would lead to more economic growth and that the share of small firms eventually would disappear or reduce to only a small fraction. Globalization has induced extensive cross-culture working ambience and driven most firms to multidimensional manufacturing and marketing operations to sustain in the competition marketplace. Hence, most firms have become increasingly complex and ungovernable, causing decline in performance, unclear accountability, and opaque decision process that raise questions on the sustainability of the firm. To avoid frustration and inefficiency, executives need to systematically address the causes of complexity using a simplicity-minded strategy in their companies by streamlining the structure, pruning nonresponding products before introducing new products to create space, building disciplined processes, and improving managerial behavior (Ashkenas 2007).

Project Lifecycle

Project lifecycle is different from the normal lifecycle of products or services as the project team faces various challenges during the process of taking the project through the stages of its lifecycle from initiation to the last stage of closing the project with profitability, market share, and consumer loyalty. Most projects encounter the market risk and uncertainty at the stage of near completion of the project, and if the project team is unable to fix these issues, it plunges in failure, creates enormous sunk cost, and thrusts on the project team to terminate it with several prejudice in an unhealthy manner. The stages of project lifecycle and their attributes are exhibited in Figure 4.2.

The classical project lifecycle has four standard stages beginning from initiation, moving to planning, then toward implementation, and finally closing, as illustrated in Figure 4.2. Project managers face conflicts of ideation, team building, resources mapping, and exploring potential for commercialization in the "initiation" stage. They appear to be lower in intensity than the "implementation" stage of the project lifecycle. At this stage, project teams undergo the major challenge of preparing work

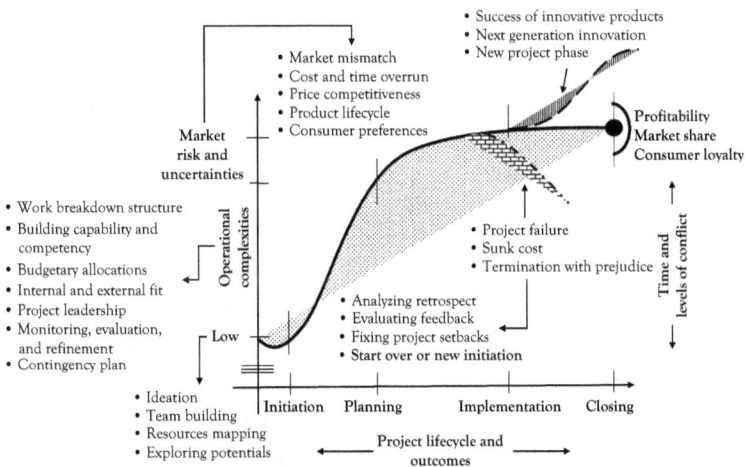

Figure 4.2 Stages, attributes, and challenges in project lifecycle

breakdown structure, making budgetary allocations, and developing contingency plan. In the "implementation" stage of innovation project, the outcomes are ready to commercialize. During the implementation stage, the major challenges with the project teams commonly emerge toward managing market mismatch with the project outcome, reducing cost and time overrun, and reorienting the innovative product to consumer preferences. The last stage of project lifecycle is closing the project with projected profitability and market share. If the project outcome is successful, companies generally start a new project of the next-generation innovation and set the new lifecycle. Contrary to this, as the project outcomes are rejected in their commercialization endeavor, they turn to fail and cause large volume of sunk cost. However, these stages are being altered time and again in the contemporary times by the market interventions and exhibit attributes other than the stages of classical project lifecycle (Westland 2006). The SUEs gather information, do crowdsourcing, develop concept, workout prototype, and test the market in the sage of "initiation" and later sell the innovation prototype and process to the large companies that intend to take up the project to the rest of the three stages.

For example, Sasken, a communication software company based in India, which provides research and development support to leading wireless device vendors from its offshore workstations in India, is engaged in continuous innovation and project development projects. Over the years, working with various innovation projects, the company has come across a number of challenges in developing an advanced multimedia player for high-end mobile handsets for the Japanese market. The project teams faced varied challenges in managing the innovation projects for different geo-demographic and market environment. The Japanese market is one of the most advanced in the mobile services it offers, and is well-ahead of the rest of the world in terms of handset functions and features. Project teams often face difficulties in managing deliverables to the clients and provide services from remote innovation centers. The Sasken project team faced a number of challenges in building a technology-intensive product according to its client's specific requirements from its offshore workstation to meet the client expectations and norms in reference to quality, completeness of the product, and timeliness of delivery. The project team also had to cope with unavailability of tools and platforms, with communication and co-ordination challenges, and with cultural differences that were typical of offshore product development (Sridhar and Vadivelu 2011).

The project manager and project team move with one shared goal in managing the project. Commonly, the projects have a linear path consisting of a beginning, a middle period during which activities move the project toward completion, and an ending with either successful or unsuccessful outcome. The project lifecycle refers to a series of activities, which are necessary to fulfill project goals or objectives. Projects vary in size and complexity, but no matter how large or small, all projects can be mapped to the following lifecycle structure:

- Starting the project
- Organizing and preparing
- Carrying out project work
- Closing the project

In the planning phase, the project is developed with comprehensive action points and maps in reference to meet the project's objective. The phases in the project planning process and their attributes are as listed as follows:

- In first phase, the team identifies task and time matrix to carry out the planned tasks. The project's tasks and resource requirements are identified in this stage of project planning by suggesting the right approaches to administer the tasks scheduled in the work breakdown structure. This phase is also referred to as "scope management."
- In the second phase, a project plan is created outlining the activities, tasks, dependencies, and timeframes. The project manager coordinates the preparation of a project budget by providing cost estimates for the labor, equipment, and materials costs. The budget is used to monitor and control cost expenditures during project implementation.
- During the third phase, the project plan is put into motion and the work of the project is performed. This phase is known as implementation phase of the project. In this phase, progress

is continuously monitored and appropriate adjustments are made and recorded as variances from the original plan. In any project, a project manager spends most of the time in this step. During project implementation, people are carrying out the tasks, and progress information is being reported through regular team meetings. The project manager uses this information to maintain control over the direction of the project by comparing the progress reports with the project plan to measure the performance of the project activities and take corrective action as needed.

• During the last phase, which is called as "closing of project," the emphasis is on releasing the final deliverables to the customer, handing over project documentation to the business, terminating supplier contracts, releasing project resources, and communicating the closure of the project to all stakeholders. Upon successful completion of the project, companies also tend to conduct "lessons-learned" studies to examine the do's and don'ts for the new projects.

Managing Competitiveness in the Innovation Projects

The market drivers of product differentiation and new products development comprise the needs of common customers, global customers, global channels, and transferable marketing. The customers' needs become a compelling factor for the multinational companies when customers of the different countries have the same needs in a product category. The free trade and unrestricted travel has created homogenous groups of customers across the countries in reference to the specific industries. However, some markets that typically deal with the culture-bound behavior and resistance of consumers toward adoption of differentiated products seek companies to offer customized products to consumers within niche. The global channels and distribution and logistics companies offer seamless transport, storage, and delivery services. Companies can expand internationally provided the channel infrastructure is met with the distribution needs of the company. Hence, their integrated networks thrive to bring new products and technologies close to the global distributors and retail stores like super markets and departmental stores in order to generate systems effect. Transferability in technology marketing is applied in congruence with the marketing ideas on brand names, packaging, advertising, and other components of marketing-mix in different countries. Nike's campaign anchoring the basketball champion Michael Jordan pulled up the brand associated with technology-led new products in many countries. This is how the good ideas of multinationals get the new technology and innovative products leveraged in the global markets (Rajagopal 2015).

The competitive drivers of product differentiation support the companies for matching their technology development and marketing strategies in accordance with the consumer preferences. The existence of global competitors indicates whether a new technology or product is ready for international business operations. Firms need to develop market infrastructure for the new technologies and products to be able to explore the scope of expansion. The competitive efforts put pressure on companies to globalize their marketing activities and derive optimum performance of the new products by interpreting appropriately the competitor signals. The cost drivers of technology and new products are largely based on the scale of economies that involve the cost of production functions in the large and complex industries, cost of outsourcing, diffusion and adaptation of technology, tariffs and taxes, and costs associated with the basic and advanced marketing functions. The macroeconomic factors of the neighboring countries also govern the cost drivers. When a new automobile plant is set up, it aims at designing, manufacturing or assembling, and delivering a particular model by penetrating into the neighboring markets to gain the advantages of economies of scale. The high market share multidomestic companies derive gains from spreading their production activities across multiple product lines or diversified business lines to achieve advantage through the scope of economies. Developing new technologies, products, manufacturing and marketing activities of Proctor and Gamble, Unilever, and Colgate-Palmolive may illustrate this global attribute that is explained by the cost drivers. Other cost drivers include global sourcing advantages, low global communications, and automation processes. The location of strategic resources to the production plants, cost differences across the countries, and transport costs are also some important considerations of the cost drivers.

The lowering of trade barriers made globalization of markets and production a theoretical possibility, and technological change has made it a tangible reality. The technology drivers play a significant role in global business. Global expansion of the multinational companies has been highly stimulated by the technological advancements in the designing, manufacturing, and marketing of consumer and industrial products. The services were also improved by many technological breakthroughs. The Internet revolution has triggered the e-commerce as open access channel that acts as a strong driving force for global business in the consumer and industry segments. Improved transport and communication now make it possible to be in continuous contact with producers anywhere in the world. This makes it easier for companies to split production of a single good over any distance. Storage and preservation techniques have revolutionized the food industry, for example, so that the idea of seasonal vegetables is no longer relevant today as anything can be exported all the year round from anywhere. Technological upgrading, in the form of introduction of new machinery and improvement of technological capabilities, provides a firm with the means to be successful in competition. In the process of introducing better technologies, new lower-cost methods become available that allow the firm to increase labor productivity, that is, the efficiency with which it converts resources into value. Firms adopt these newer methods of production if they are more profitable than the older ones. The ability of a firm to take advantage of technical progress is also enhanced if the firm improves its entrepreneurial and technological capabilities through two competitive strategies, namely learning and adaptation strategy and innovation strategy. The latter is a process of searching for, finding, developing, imitating, adapting, and adopting new products, new processes, and new organizational arrangements. Because rivals do not stand still, the firm's capacity to develop these capabilities, as well as its ability to compete depends on the firm's maintaining a steady pace of innovation (Asian Development Bank 2003). Containerization has revolutionized the transportation business, significantly lowering the costs of shipping goods over long distances. Before the advent of containerization, moving goods from one mode of transport to another was very labor-intensive, lengthy, and costly. It could take days to unload a ship and reload goods onto trucks and trains. The efficiency gains associated with containerization and transportation costs have fallen, making it much more economical to ship goods around the world to drive the globalization. The government drivers for the globalization include diplomatic trade relations, custom unions, or common markets.

Communication is another important driver of innovation and differentiation. Mass media channels are the most rapid and efficient means of communicating to a large number of potential adopters, but interpersonal communication is more effective in persuading potential adopters to accept a new idea. Direct communication among users of the same socioeconomic segment and educational level increases the potential of acceptance even more. Although scholarly writings and curriculum resources provide an abundance of information about the effectiveness and benefits of media literacy training, a majority of potential adopters will be more influenced by conversations with their peers.

The most evident reason to drive the companies go global is the market potential in the developing countries that act as major players in the world market. Companies such as Nintendo, Disney, and the Japanese motorcycle industries have been greatly benefited from exploiting the markets of the developing countries and reassuring their growth in the world market to harness the promising market potential. The emerging scope of spatial diversification has also been one of the drivers for enhancement of the global business, utilizing the additional production capacity at the economies of scale and low-cost outsourcing. The saturation of demand for the products and services of a company in the domestic market may also be an effective driver to globalization, wherein the company looks for building value for its brand across the boundaries. A product that is near the end of its lifecycle in the domestic market begins to generate growth abroad. Sometimes, the cross-cultural attributes of overseas markets become the source of new product ideation. Such backward sourcing of technology insights may also be considered as one of the potential drivers for globalization of business and exploring the strategic alliances with prominent regional or multinational brands thereof.

Successful consumer-led products in the competitive marketplace always try to gain a distinct place among competing firms and focus on acquiring new customers and retaining the existing ones. Repeat buying behavior of customers is largely determined by the values acquired on the product. The attributes, awareness, trial, availability, and repeat factors influence the customers toward making rebuying decisions in reference to the marketing strategies of the firm. The perception on repeat buying is affected by the level of satisfaction derived from the buying experience of customers (Rajagopal and Rajagopal 2008). Among growing competition in retailing consumer products, innovative point of sales promotions offered by super markets are aimed at boosting sales and augmenting the store brand value. Purchase acceleration and product trial are found to be the two most influential variables of retail point of sales promotions. Analysis of five essential qualities of customer value judgment in terms of interest, subjectivity, exclusivity, thoughtfulness, and internality, need to be carried out in order to make the firm customer-centric and its strategies touching bottom of the pyramid (Dobson 2007). Dynamic complexity in a business may arise in oligopolistic market systems with high risk in investment, brand development, and generative customer loyalty. It may be observed that the switching behavior of consumers occur when the distribution of a company is weak in the market. In many cases, companies are not able to carry out controlled experiments on implementing business strategies due to cost-related and ethical reasons. Hence, dynamic complexity not only slows the learning loop, but also reduces the learning gained on each cycle. Developing right business strategies in a right market situation is a growing challenge among the systems thinkers and business strategists. Delays in developing appropriate strategy create instability in market dynamic systems and adds negative feedback loops in the market, which reduces the sustainability of the company in the competitive marketplace.

The firm's decision to add a product to the line is influenced by its compatibility with reference to marketing, finances, and environment. Marketing competitiveness involves the match between the new addition and the current and potential marketing compatibilities of the parent company and its foreign subsidiary in matters such as product, price, promotion, and distribution. The firm needs to analyze the risks pertaining to financial operations and opportunities related to the addition of a new product line, which the firm is looking for. The common criteria in determining the financial compatibility of the proposed addition may be the profitability and cash flow implications. Besides, to ensure that the newly added product line would not encounter any legal and political problems, it is required for the firm to analyze the factors of environmental compatibility, which includes concern for the customer, competitive action, and legal or political problems. The inclusion of a product in the line should not pose any problem for either the existing or potential customers (Rajagopal 2014).

References

Abbott, P., Y. Zheng, and R. Du. 2013. "Innovation Through Collaborative Partnerships: Creating the MSN News iPad App at VanceInfo Technologies." *Journal of Information Technology* 3, no. 1, pp. 16–28.

Argyris, C. 1998. "Empowerment: The Emperor's New Clothes." *Harvard Business Review* 76, no. 3, pp. 98–105.

Ashkenas, R. 2007. "Simplicity Minded Management." *Harvard Business Review* 85, no. 12, pp. 101–9.

Asian Development Bank. 2003. "Drivers of Change, Globalization, Technology and Competition." Section III Competitiveness in Developing Asia. *Asian Development Outlook*. Asian Development Bank. Bangkok.

Bettencourt, L.A., and A.W. Ulwick. 2008. "The Customer-Centered Innovation Map." *Harvard Business Review* 86, no. 5, pp. 109–14.

Cash, J.I., M.J. Earl, and R. Morison. 2008. "Teaming Up to Crack Innovation and Enterprise Integration." *Harvard Business Review* 86, no. 10, pp. 90–99.

Chaudhry, A.S. August 14–18, 2005. "Knowledge Sharing Practices in Asian Institutions: A Multi-Cultural Perspective from Singapore." In *Proceedings of 71th IFLA General Conference and Council*. Oslo, Norway.

De Meyer, A., C.H. Loch, and M.T. Pich. 2002. "Managing Project Uncertainty: From Variation to Chaos." *MIT Sloan Management Review* 43, no. 2, pp. 60–67.

Dobson, J. 2007. "Aesthetics as a Foundation for Business Activity." *Journal of Business Ethics* 72, no. 1, pp. 41–46.

Gottfredson, M., and K. Aspinall. 2005. "Innovation Versus Complexity: What Is Too Much of a Good Thing?" *Harvard Business Review* 83, no. 11, pp. 62–71.

Gottfredson, M., and A. Schwedel. August 01, 2008. "Cut Complexity and Costs." *Harvard Business Publishing Newsletters*. Cambridge, MA: Harvard Business School Press.

Gratton, L. November 01, 2007. "Four Ways to Encourage More Productive Teamwork." *Harvard Business Publishing Newsletters*, Cambridge, MA: Harvard Business School.

Gupta, A.K., and V. Govindarajan. 2000. "Knowledge Management's Social Dimension: Lessons from Nucor Steel." *MIT Sloan Management Review* 42, no. 1, pp. 71–80.

Hong, D., E. Suh, and V. Koo. 2011. "Developing Strategies for Overcoming Barriers to Knowledge Sharing Based on Conversational Knowledge Management: A Case Study of a Financial Company." *Expert Systems with Applications* 38, no. 12, pp. 14417–27.

Johnson, G., G.S. Yip, and M. Hensmans. 2012. "Achieving Successful Strategic Transformation." *MIT Sloan Management Review* 53, no. 3, pp. 25–32.

Kayes, D.C., D. Stirling, and T.M. Nielsen. 2007. "Building Organizational Integrity." *Business Horizons* 50, no. 1, pp. 61–70.

Leonard-Barton, D., H.K. Bowen, K.B. Clark, C.A. Holloway, and S.C. Wheelwright. 1994. "How to Integrate Work and Deepen Expertise." *Harvard Business Review* 72, no. 5, pp. 121–30.

Pascale, R.T., and J. Sternin. 2005. "Your Company's Secret Change Agents." *Harvard Business Review* 83, no. 5, pp. 72–81.

Pinto, J.K., and O.P. Kharbanda. 1996. "How to Fail in Project Management (Without Really Trying)." *Business Horizons* 39, no. 4, pp. 45–53.

Qu, H., B. Ryan, and R. Chu. 2001. "The Perceived Importance of Job Attributes Among Foodservice Employees in Hong Kong Hotel Industry." *International Journal of Hospitality and Tourism Administration* 2, no. 2, pp. 57–76.

Rajagopal. 2014. *Architecting Enterprise: Managing Innovation, Technology, and Global Competitiveness.* Hampshire, Basingstoke, UK: Palgrave Macmillan.

Rajagopal. 2015. *Butterfly Effect in Competitive Markets: Driving Small Change for Larger Differences.* Basingstoke, Hampshire, UK: Palgrave Macmillan.

Rajagopal, and A. Rajagopal. 2008. "Team Performance and Control Process in Sales Organizations." *Team Performance Management* 14, no. 1, pp. 70–85.

Sarkees, M., and S. Hulland. 2008. "Innovation and Efficiency: It is possible to Have it All." *Business Horizons* 52, no. 1, pp. 45–55.

Sridhar, V., and S. Vedivelu. 2011. *Challenges in Developing Products for an Advanced Mobile Market: Sasken's Experience.* Cambridge, MA: Harvard Business School Press.

Thurm, D. 2005. "Master of the House: Why a Company Should Take Control of Its Building Projects." *Harvard Business Review* 83, no. 10, pp. 120–29.

van Stel, A., and V. Stunnenberg. 2006. "Linking Business Ownership and Perceived Administrative Complexity." *Journal of Small Business and Enterprise Development* 13, no. 1, pp. 7–22.

Vermeulen, F., P. Puranam, and R. Gulati. 2010. "Change for Change's Sake." *Harvard Business Review* 88, no. 6, pp. 70–76.

Westland, J. 2006. *The Project Management Lifecycle: A complete Step-by-Step Methodology for Initiating, Planning, Executing, and Closing a Project Successfully.* London: Kogan Page.

CHAPTER 5

Administering Business Projects

Overview

Administering innovative business projects is often a complex problem. Hence, there is growing demand for new approaches among companies to support the performance of business projects and organizational structure. The project administration practices have spawned innovative processes from both manufacturers and project designers. Consequently, a multitude of new concepts and processes in administering innovative business projects have emerged in the 21st century. New products, technologies, and concepts are frequently implemented in the business projects with high-level organizational support. This chapter discusses the right perspectives of setting scope of the project and developing work breakdown structure (WBS) to manage cost and time resources. This chapter would benefit managers in making spatial and temporal adjustments in the business projects and carrying out network analysis. The approaches for managing the business projects through the stage-gate process, and effective monitoring and evaluation to protect the business projects from falling into the black holes have been discussed comprehensively in this chapter.

Administering innovative business projects are complex and sensitive to the cost, time, and quality risks of deliverables. The most crucial tasks in project administration include developing a project charter, project scope and scope creep, managing cost and time using critical path method (CPM), deliverables, and commercialization of the project outcome. Often innovative business projects are terminated prematurely as the project deliverables do not match the current market demand. Consumer preferences and requirements of the sponsors often change during midproject, causing delay or termination of the projects. However, risk management can only manage known risks, but uncertainties in project operations might cause damage to the projects in terms of cost, time, and deliverables. Every project has some known or unknown risks or both. The techniques of conventional risk management apply only to the known risks. Large, complex projects are difficult to administer due to scope creep, technology shifts, instability in the project teams, and change of leadership. Thus, project administration becomes difficult, and the increase in encountering risks, becomes more likely. The projects turn cumbersome when there are additional tasks in the project to be performed within the budgetary constraints. The more complicated a project seems to the project manager and other participants, the greater the likelihood that something important will be missed, thus increasing the likelihood of redoing tasks in the project by borrowing more time and delaying the completion of the project (Browning and Ramasesh 2015).

Project Scope

Managing innovation projects and achieving commercial success is often not a guaranteed mission. The innovation projects appear to be fragile as they have to pass through risk, and uncertainties concerning human and capital resources, and market behavior. The innovation projects can be successful, provided the companies should establish the projects with sound mission and scope frameworks. Developing an effective project scope is a process, which helps to decide whether or not to proceed with the project. An incomplete emphasis of the project scope often throws inordinate difficulties in the early stages of a project's lifecycle, as such situation in the project affects the execution of tasks. Meanwhile, the project team can map the tasks and outcomes by stages of the projects and fix accountabilities among the members of the teams understanding variabilities of interests. Innovation projects, in specific, bring different degrees of changes on the surrounding environment and people involved in the project. Therefore, leaders of innovation projects should redefine the project scope and boundaries subjected to changing outcomes, market demand, and expectation of different stakeholders (Fageha and Aibinu 2013). Project scope is defined as the process of the work to be performed in order to deliver a product, service, or result with the specified features and functions. The project scope is dependent on the project outcome as product or service, which defines its features and functions. Thus, project scope management ensures that both the outcome of the project and the project scope are periodically monitored and properly maintained. It is important to establish the project objectives, which include a new product, creating a new service within the organization to frame the project scope in a right way. There are a number of objectives that could be central to a project that might influence laying out the project scope. However, it is critical for the project manager to ensure that the team delivers the project results within the project scope.

The scope of a project is the clear path of the work required to successfully complete or deliver a project. The project manager should ensure that only the required work that delineates the scope is performed to complete the project within time and budget limits by providing all deliverables to the stakeholders. The documentation of the scope of the project explains the limits of the project, fixes accountability of each member of the team, and clearly lays the procedures for performing tasks that are approved by the project leader and disseminated down to the team members working on the project. The standard project methodology suggests that the project scope should be defined before rolling out the task to be performed by the teams. Collaboration among the project owner including the start-up enterprises (SUEs), regional firms, or large companies, sponsor, and stakeholders not only guides the project toward delivering outcomes, but also helps in developing the right scope of the project. The scope must make clear to all involved in the project exactly what product or service needs to be delivered upon completion of the project. A good project continues to accomplish its goals with the established and approved project scope. Making changes in the scope during the midproject is called as scope creep. Finally, the project manager defines project scope by identifying what initiated the request for a desired project outcome in terms of either an innovative product or service, or both.

The scope of the project should be developed before developing the WBS to avoid any abrupt changes in the task, time, cost, and accountability criteria in the middle of the project. Any changes in the project tasks would shift all financial and operational parameters of the project and such changes are referred as "scope creep." As the scope changes affect the project, project managers often try to redefine the critical path to reach the project goal by skipping or combining a few tasks that might cause cost and time overrun and divert the project from the predetermined path. Some of the costs of scope creep may derive the following outcomes:

- Deferred benefits
- Lowered return on investment
- Increased maintenance costs
- Overallocated staff
- New risks

The project creep becomes necessary in the project due to market uncertainties and the changes in the availability of project resources or the corporate policies toward the innovation projects. The project managers can accordingly consider the project scope creep over the original project plan. It is not unusual to anticipate changes in the original project plan as the project work advances, which forces project managers to redefine the project scope. However, implementation of change management tools within the organization discourages the managers to make changes in the project scope. An effective change management team would be able to control both internally generated and customer-driven changes in the scope of projects and reduce the scope creep impact. In order to incorporate customer-driven changes and modify the project scope strategy, the customer often participates as a member of the project team to guide the required change. The role of customers in managing the project scope creep addresses how the change will affect the project budget as well as assignment of cost-task-risk, and staff allocations. Some tools and techniques useful in capturing the project scope are discussed as follows:

- Define the project need
- Identify key stakeholders
- Identify project drivers
- Develop operational concepts
- Identify external interfaces

The project scope should be developed in a way that it is compatible to the project charter and the WBS. The general practice of project management suggests that developing the project scoping and its process is all about developing an initial WBS, which is a result-oriented family tree of the project cost, tasks, and time allocations, risk factors, and anticipated outcomes at each stage of the project. The project scope in convergence with the WBS exhibits all the potential work to be done in the project in an organized way. It is often portrayed graphically as a hierarchical tree with a list of element categories and tasks. The WBS makes large complex innovation projects more systematic to work by progressively smaller work packages that may include a number of tasks. Upon drawing proper application of the project scope management, it helps effectively in managing the critical factors of project management such as cost, time, risk, quality, and outcomes. Besides the critical project factors, the scope management also provides support in managing the following external dimensions:

- Helps in management of projects belonging to public (government) and private organizations
- Helps in prioritizing and reducing the temporary work requests, which can save time and cost
- Allows project teams to conduct cost-benefit analysis to validate the need for any deviations in the project path in reference to WBS and scope creep in the middle of the innovation projects
- Facilitates productive communications with stakeholders and among the team
- Serves as a tool to manage client expectations, work load balancing, and team morale

Project *scope verification* is interwoven with project planning phases and process stage-gates. It provides an opportunity for the client to review the performance after some of the initial work has been done, and verify that the work is of acceptable quality and further tasks can be carried out as per the project plan. The scope verification is needed in an innovation project to determine whether to stay with the predetermined task in the project plan and to avoid any overlap or deviation of the tasks. Thus, the project scope verification is a random process to be carried out many times during the project process. The scope creep in an innovation project is commonly considered after acquiring the review of customers on the product concept or prototype for making desired modification in the end product before commercialization. If the end users prefer to suggest modifications to be done in the end product, the proposed changes should be evaluated in reference to technological feasibility and economic viability, prior to making changes in the project scope. The purpose of reviewing the project scope creep is to keep the goals of end users and the company as close to the cost-time-risk (CTR) plans as possible, and enhancing the market potential for the final deliverables. This phase of the project scope is designed to strengthen and reinforce the initial scope definition through feedback. However, scope changes in innovation projects are common and often inevitable, as market players involved with the project often reset their business goals. At this point, the concept of scope creep is introduced in a project, subject to approval of the project leader and to restrict any unauthorized changes. If the project team does not control the scope creep in the project, the potential consequences of scope change may result into premature termination of the project, market failure, and heavy sunk cost, leading to irrecoverable loss to the company. A change control should be managed by the project team through formal documentation that provides statements about any changes in project scope to guide the process as smoothly as possible. A scope change control should be put in place in the project path as early as possible to synchronize with the existing tasks to be performed and classify the types of changes suggested by the market players. Changes in scope can have a great effect on every element considering the minimum variations in the CTR factors by defining the changes in an orderly fashion to keep the end users and market players involved in the project activities. However, accommodating new requests becomes more expensive due to changes in the cost and risk parameters in the market. The successful projects manage the creep from the beginning, considering the potential returns on investment and market value. One of the most damaging aspects of scope creep is the increasing project cost, as it not only drains the project budget by adding new tasks and work packages, but also adds time to tasks that pushes back completion dates, causing a loss in the potential profits that would have been realized with an on time completion of the project. Scope creep can also create a larger and more complex end result that costs more to maintain upon commercializing the outcome of the project. Figure 5.1 exhibits the internal and external situations that make the project team implement project scope creep.

The scope creep in a project is driven by the changing demand of consumers and market players including sponsors, distributors, and retailers, as illustrated in Figure 5.1. The project team evaluates the requirements to accommodate the change by creating additional tasks (T6A, T7A...) in the WBS in order to improve the shareholder value. The project scope creep throws several effects on the innovation project, which include cost and time exigencies, cost of team training to manage additional tasks, and the risk of quality of project deliverables. The project might also suffer from the risk of cost and time overrun, and quality of deliverable in implementing the additional tasks created and making them compatible with the project goals and outcomes. The scope creep in a project might cause changes in the attributes *deliverables, uncertainty* in performing the additional tasks, *cost* escalation, and *time* prolongation (DUCT). Thus, the project team should carefully evaluate the need for scope creep before introducing the additional tasks in addition to the mainstream project scope.

In order to manage the scope creep in a project, it is necessary to have streamlined communication among the project teams internally, and with the stakeholders externally to smoothen the deviations of tasks emerging due to the scope creep. The changes adding features and functionality to the scope of the project without communicating through the proper channels and getting the proper authorizations could not be implemented. Regularly communicating the progress of the project to team members and stakeholders will not only help the project team manage the tasks efficiently, but will also prevent scope creep. Also, communicating the status of open issues will also keep scope creep in check, as the team members and stakeholders are aware of the roles and responsibilities in addressing these issues. The communication with the project can be managed through the networks consisting a set of core team members who bring noncore contributors within the communication gamut and share

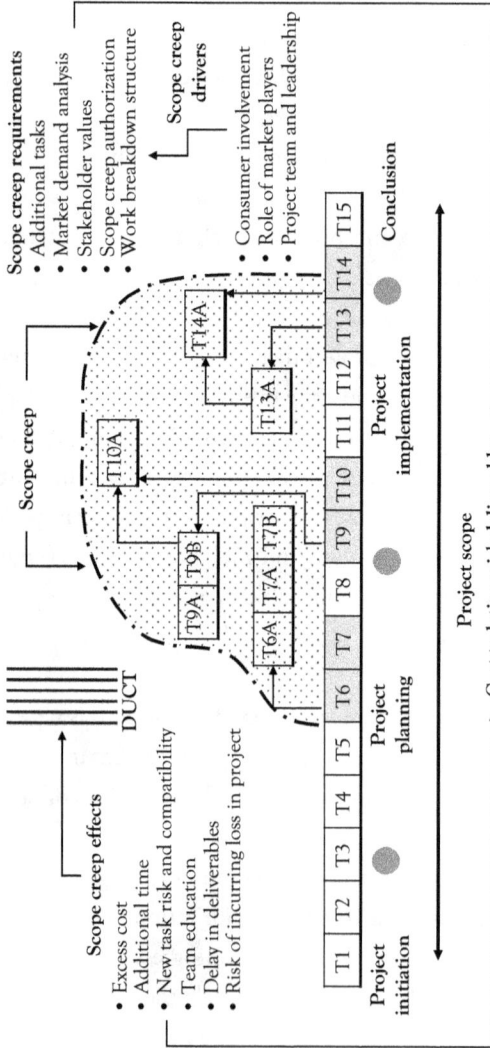

Figure 5.1 Scope creep in innovation projects: attributes and effects

knowledge, information, and feedback regarding the team's task. A project network can be helpful when the project scope is beyond control, the sphere of influence of the core team is not uniform, the task is complex, and it is unclear to reach an optimal solution. Managers can use a project's kick-off meeting to set norms and project scope to reach the desired expectation on the project and as an option to look outside the team for possible solutions to complex problems (Cummings and Peltcher 2011).

Project Charter

In project management, a project charter is a complete document that presents the objectives, scope, task schedule, team and stakeholders, risk management, deliverables, and approvals. It provides a preliminary delineation of roles and responsibilities, outlines the project objectives, identifies the main stakeholders, and defines the authority of the project manager. The terms of reference are usually part of the project charter. The project charter formally and holistically describes the project, authorizes a project or a specific project phase, and it is used as tool for kickoff by the project sponsor. It is a very powerful document as it assures the proper visibility of the project by defining the roles and responsibilities within the project and aligns the project to the strategic goals and objectives of the organization. A good project charter should include the following attributes:

- Executive summary
  - Project justification
  - Project purpose
  - Project scope—description of tasks that are included and excluded in the project
  - Project deliverables, outcome, and completion goals
  - Critical success factors, team constitution, and stakeholder summary
  - Co-creation, stakeholder involvement, attributes of sponsor, and market behavior
  - Major milestones in the project
  - Risk, contingencies, and situational management

- Purpose of the project
  - Role of project charter for the project leader and team members
  - Corporate objectives and goals
  - Compatibility of project deliverables with corporate goals
  - Enhancing corporate identity, brand image, and customer value
- Project justification
  - Uniqueness
  - Compatibility with the market needs
  - Business case
- Project scope
  - Scope definition, project boundaries, and roles of team members and project leader
  - Project constraints
  - Critical success factors
- Project schedule
  - Project process, completion, and task distribution
  - WBS, and work packages
  - CTR-deliverables matrix
  - Cost and time overrun estimates, and contingency plans
- Team and stakeholders
  - Project team and leadership profiles
  - Project sponsor profiles
  - Goals, accountability, and task administration

Specifically, a project charter provides the project manager the power to bring the project team together to accomplish the task of completing the project successfully. Project managers still face many resource challenges, depending on the structure of the project. However, a properly developed project charter that is communicated to the project sponsor and stakeholders enables the project manager to organize the team work to match with the expectations and responsibilities of the sponsors and stakeholders. The project cannot be is technically authorized until the project charter is completed and authorized. The project charter should provide information on the following points:

- *Project identification* including the title of the project and brief description of the project along with the particulars of the project team.
- *Project objectives* in reference to predetermined project benefits to the organization, ways of aligning project with the strategic priorities of the organization, expected outcome, deliverables, and benefits to be realized.
- *Assumptions* made in the decision to charter this project. All assumptions must be validated to ensure that the project stays on schedule and within the budgetary provisions.
- *Project scope* to establish the boundaries of the project in order to identify the limits of the project and define the deliverables. Any requirements that are specifically excluded from the project scope should also be listed.
- Major *milestones* and deliverables of the project according to the schedule of date.
- List of the *potential impacts* the project may have on existing systems or units.
- *Project resources* comprising initial funding, personnel, and other resources committed to this project by the project sponsor.
- High-level *project risks* and the strategies to mitigate them.
- *Metrics* to project success and describe that the project team is trying to achieve as a project outcome.
- *Roles and responsibilities* of project team members followed by the names and contact information for those filling the roles in tabular form. Modifies, overwritten, and other examples must be added to accurately describe the roles and responsibilities of the team members. The roles and responsibilities of the stakeholders (consumers) and, subject experts if any, working with the project must be described.
  - The role and responsibility of the sponsor include to approve the project charter and plan, secure resources for the project, confirm the project's goals and objectives, keep abreast of major project activities, make decisions on escalated issues, and assist in the resolution of roadblocks.

o A project manager leads in the planning and development of the project and manages the project to scope. His role and responsibilities include developing the project plan, identifying project deliverables, risks, and developing a risk management plan. A project manager is also responsible for directing the project team, developing the project scope, administer process control and change management, ensure quality assurance during the project process, and maintain all documentation including the project plan. The project manager also needs to report and forecast project status to the project sponsor, resolve conflicts within the project or between cross-functional teams, and make sure that the project outcomes would meet the business objectives. A project leader also communicates periodically the project status to stakeholders.

o The team members work toward the deliverables of the project. The members of the project team conduct initial research on the project backward and forward linkages, and collect and analyze the data as outlined in the project plan. The project team also liaisons with the project manager about the scope of the project, risk and quality concerns, and proactively involve in managing project outcomes and expectations.

A project charter should contain the essence of the project, provide a shared understanding of the project, and act as a contract between the project sponsor, key stakeholders, and the project team. The project charter is usually a short document that refers to more detailed documents, such as a new offering request or a request for proposal.

In innovative projects management, companies develop Initiative for Policy Dialogue (IPD) by documenting all the necessary attributes to carry out the project with initial observation and discussion with the project teams. This document serves as a project charter. The innovation project management leaders will also develop customer preference and value (CPV) matrix and construct the critical definitions in the project accordingly. Both IPD and CPV serve as the integral part of the project management process. The project charter establishes the authority assigned to the project manager, especially in a matrix management environment, which includes decision grid among various project subleaders like engineering, manufacturing, testing, marketing, finance, administration, and research and development. Such matrix project system explained in the project charter is considered as the best practice within the industry. The principal uses of the project charter include:

- Provide a comparable format for ranking the projects
- Draw cost-benefit analysis and authorize the time, tasks, and deliverables in reference to the value approximation of the returns on investment
- Serve as the primary document for the project for commercialization of innovation in reference to the stakeholder value
- Serve as a guiding tool throughout the project and determine the baselines that can be used in team management, monitoring and control, and managing the project scope

For a large multiphased and multi-layered innovation project, the charter can be created for each individual phase or layer. The project layer is considered as scaling-up the performance of tasks in reference to technology upgrades and business analytics. Such layered project consumes more time in performing each task, as the project team needs to trained for each task or phase of the project. In a multilayered project, the project team can develop an initial charter during the scope phase of a project, followed by a planning charter, and an execution charter during at the operational phase of the project. Developing the charter and identifying the stakeholders are the two major concerns in managing an innovation project. The project charter can be documented by using the following resources:

- Project "Statement of Work"
- Business case
- Work agreements and operations alliances with external agencies
- Enterprise standards, industry standards, regulations, and norms
- Organizational process, assets, and templates

Typically, the project manager takes lead in developing the charter in association with the area-specific team members. The project manager works with the key stakeholders, that is, customers and business sponsors, subject-matter experts inside and outside the organization, intra-organization departments, various business groups within the industry, and professional bodies like Project Management Institute to develop the project charter. The project manager employs facilitation techniques such as brainstorming, problem solving, conflict resolution, meetings, expectations management, and so on, to develop the charter. The charter once signed provides authority to the project manager to officially execute the project and employ organizational funds and resources to make the project successful.

Innovation Lifecycle

Innovation lifecycle moves through common lifecycle comprising introduction, growth, maturity, and decline in the context of market behavior. However, the attributes of innovation cycle in different stages vary from the product or organization lifecycles to some extent. Innovation cycle cannot be determined in general as it differs for the types of innovation and its growth in the market conditions. The innovation drivers in reference to its backward and forward linkages, unique proposition, innovation value, and high investment to carry out product innovation occur during the introduction stage of the innovation lifecycle. Firms foster the strategies of 4As to strengthen the product awareness, acceptance, availability, and affordability in order to reduce the market risk and gain competitive advantage of the new product in the marketplace. As the innovative products move to the growth stage, firms put more impetus on sales by refining the marketing-mix strategies in reference to the following elements consisting of 11 Ps (Rajagopal 2012):

- Product (uniqueness and associated attributes that distinguish the product from the existing products in a given marketplace)
- Price (low-end or premium market pricing)
- Place (developing strategies on distribution management and routes to market in reference to make the product available at the convenience of consumers)

- Promotion (developing promotion packages, advertisement and communication strategies, and building product opinions among consumers and market players)
- Packaging
- Pace (time)
- People (front-line employees of an organization engaged in selling the product)
- Performance (product performance and consumer experience)
- Psychodynamics (consumers engaged in social media to share their experience on the innovative product)
- Posture (corporate image)
- Proliferation (expansion into manufacturing and launching complimentary products to augment the use value of the innovation)

At the *growth* stage of innovation, the threats of value disruption due to negative word-of-mouth and competitive tactics in the market against the product are often observed by the firms that increase the risk of substitution and consumer defection. Innovation-led products are also susceptible to imitations by infringement of intellectual property rights and disruptive technologies with the increase of market competition against the innovative product. Most firms invest in building product brands at this stage and enhance services support to inculcate confidence among the consumers and augment their loyalty toward the product and company.

Innovation-led products turn sustainable in the *maturity* stage as they gain the desired market share and position them strategically with long-term goals in the market competition. In this stage, both the consumer value and brand equity for the innovation-led products and services increase. However, as the technology grows and consumer preferences for the products change over time, the products turn obsolete in the *decline* stage, depleting their market share and increasing the substitution risk. Firms, thus, should be engaged in continuous improvement or innovation process to develop next-generation products at the edge of the mature stage and avoid falling in to the *decline* stage. Products, which fall into the decline stage, are difficult to revive as the dynamic market forces weaken the product significance and turn them idle in the marketplace.

Often investing on the products trapped in the decline stage does not yield expected returns and turns into sunk cost that cannot be recovered.

Product innovation and marketing cycle are also affected by the innovation diffusion cycle spread across the same stages as of product innovation cycle. In the introduction stage, often the diffusion of information is low, as firms do not employ adequate resources in generating awareness on the innovation. Firms invite lead users in this stage to test the innovated product and influence early adopters on the usage of product. Lead users form a small group, but act as powerful referral and brand carriers. Firms spend adequate resources in the growth stage to diffuse product innovation attributes through direct communication on one-on-one basis to drive intensive effect on the innovation-led products among early adopters. Consumers in this group are strong followers of lead users and stand as effective opinion leaders for influencing the early majority of consumers. Most companies deploy enormous resources in advertising, communication, and social media involvement during the late growth and maturity stages to drive customers who are less affluent and less educated, but ready to experiment with the innovative products. The early majority consumer segment constitutes relatively larger than the previous consumer segments but is confined to niche. The following is late majority segment, which is a very large segment and often represents about half of the total number of consumers in a given market area. This consumer segment exhibits high adaptability with the innovative products and derives satisfactory value for money that makes the late majority consumers frequent buyers. Consumers in this segment are price-sensitive and pose the threat of defection when more attractive substitute products penetrate into the market. However, a small number of (about 20 percent) of consumers in each market segment are hard to drive for buying any innovative product as they are indecisive and difficult to convince. Such segment of consumers is found in all stages of growth of innovative products, but is apparently huge in the decline stage of the product lifecycle.

An individual's choice of innovative organic products can be linked clearly to ethical stances, but ethical choices can also vary from individual to individual, from industry to industry, and among countries. Consumer purchasing motivations are revealed in a study as being self-interest-centered rather than altruistic. Hence, to enhance the scope of organic products marketing in future, the firms must aim to modify perceptions and attitudes of larger consumer segments by implementing educational marketing campaigns that reinforce the ethical, environmental, and societal benefits of organic production. The key challenge for organic products marketers is to strengthen individuals' perception of the individual benefits by adding more and stronger emotional values to green brands. Future green marketing research should extend its analysis to the emotional motivations and benefits associated with environmentally responsible consumption behavior (Hartmann and Apaolaza 2006). The green intentions of organic products significantly influence ethnocentrism, environmental concern, involvement, and attitudes. However, risk aversion has been found as the major emerging variable, while involvement and environmental concern are significant in determining the consumer behavior toward organic products (Paladino 2005). Concerns related to the environment are evident in the increasingly ecologically conscious marketplace. It has been observed in one of the research studies that females, married and with at least one child living at home, are the consumers who are willing to pay more for environmentally friendly products. They place a high importance on security and warm relationships with others, and they often consider ecological issues when making a purchase (Laroche, Bergeron, and Barbaro-Forleo 2001).

Among information technology (IT) companies, Google stands out as an enterprise designed with the explicit goal of succeeding at rapid, profuse innovation. Much of what the company does is rooted in its legendary IT infrastructure, but technology and strategy at Google are inseparable and mutually permeable, making it hard to say whether technology is the DNA of its strategy or the other way around. Google has spent billions of dollars in creating its Internet-based operating platform and developing proprietary technology that allows the company to rapidly develop and roll out new services of its own or of a business partner. As owner and operator of its innovation "ecosystem," Google can control the platform's evolution and claim a disproportionate percentage of the value created within it. Because every transaction is performed through the platform, the company has perfect, continuous awareness of, and access to the by-product information and is the hub of all germinal revenue streams. In addition to the technology explicitly designed and built for innovation, Google has a well-considered organizational and cultural strategy that helps the company attract the most talented people in the world and keep them working hard. For instance, Google budgets innovation into job descriptions and eliminates friction from development processes, and tries to learn from failures and chaos. However, some elements of Google's success as an innovator are very hard and expensive (Iyer and Davenport 2008).

It is also possible for a firm to penetrate into the market faster and outperform the close competing products that exist, if the ex-factory market dynamics is comparatively faster. We may define such dynamics as escape velocity for the new products, which manifests in increasing the customer value, market coverage, just-in-time supply management, and augmenting product performance through in-store and point-of-sales demonstrations. It is observed that the faster the market penetration of new products, the higher the opportunity of market coverage over the competing product in a given time and territory. The new product attractiveness may comprise the product features, including improved attributes, use of advance technology, innovativeness, extended product applications, brand augmentation, perceived use value, competitive advantages, corporate image, product advertisements, sales and services policies associated therewith, which contribute in building sustainable customer values toward making buying decisions on the new products. The introduction of new technological products makes it important for marketers to understand how innovators or first adopters respond to persuasion cues. It has been observed in a study that the innovativeness and perceived product newness, which are one of the constituents of new product attractiveness, are independent constructs that had independent effects on customer's attitude toward the brand and purchase intent for the new product. The attractiveness of new products is one of the key factors affecting the decision making of customers, and is turn related to market growth and sales. The higher the positive reactions of the customers toward the new products in view of their attractiveness, the higher the growth in sales and so in market (Lafferty and Goldsmith 2004).

Customer involvement in developing new products has been widely used in American and Japanese manufacturing firms. Quality Function

Deployment (QFD) is uses as the most popular tool for bringing the voice of the customer into the product development process from conceptual design through manufacturing. The process of QFD begins with a matrix that links customer-desired product engineering requirements, along with competitive benchmarking information, and further matrices can be used to ultimately link this to design of the manufacturing system. Unlike other methods originally developed in the United States and transferred to Japan, the QFD methodology was born out of Total Quality Control (TQC) activities in Japan during the 1960s and has been transferred to companies in the United States. It has been observed that the companies in the United States showed a higher degree of usage, management support, cross-functional involvement, use of QFD-driven data sources, and perceived benefits from using QFD. These companies are more suitable to use newly collected customer data sources, such as focus groups and methods, for analyzing customer requirements. Japanese companies have been found using the existing product services data like implications of guarantee, warranty, and a broader set of matrixes. The use of analytical techniques in conjunction with QFD including simulation, design of experiments, regression, mathematical target setting, and analytic hierarchy process are also considered as supporting tools for analyzing customer data (Cristiano, Liker, and White 2000). Similarly, recent studies have described how "lean" Japanese car assemblers assigned the design and development of whole modules to a group of first-tier suppliers, who in turn utilized a team of second-tier suppliers for the detailed development and engineering. Customer-involved product development strategies were also found to be common with the firms in different industries, including Apple, Benetton, Corning, McDonald's, Nike, Nintendo, Sun, and Toyota. The customer firm, often a large original equipment manufacturer, perceives that its power may be cascaded throughout its supply base. At the basic level, cascading is a way for a customer to delegate responsibility to its suppliers. In practice, it has been contended that cascading more often takes the form of a more imposing style of leadership (Lamming et al. 2000). Along with the factors of QFD, companies should also develop the product innovation charter, considering the following critical variables in new product development process:

- Core competencies
  - Quality, function, delivery, infrastructure—4As (attributes, awareness, availability, and affordability) and 11 Ps (including product, price, place, promotion, packaging, pace, people, performance, psychodynamics, posture, and proliferation)
  - Technology, product experience, customer franchise, end user experience
- Technology derives
  - Technological strengths, global competition, nonlaboratory technology, small-order-handling technology
- Market drivers
  - Dual-drive strategy, co-producer (customer—focus), mass customization, distributors
- Technical driver together with a market driver
- Technology of microfilming and the market activity of education
- Global satellite technology and golf course superintendents
- Goals and objectives
  - Profit, growth, market status

In the Internet age, firms are recognizing the power of the Internet as a platform for co-creating value with customers. Internet has impacted the process of collaborative innovation as a key process in value co-creation. Distinctive capabilities of the Internet as a platform for customer engagement, including interactivity, enhanced reach, persistence, speed, and flexibility, suggest that firms can use these capabilities to engage customers in collaborative product innovation through a variety of Internet-based mechanisms. The network mechanisms can facilitate collaborative innovation at different stages of the new product development process (backend versus frontend stages) and for different levels of customer involvement (high reach versus high richness). Ducati, a manufacturer of motorbikes, and Eli Lilly, a multinational pharmaceutical company, are found to be actively engaged in encouraging customer involvement in developing new products (Sawhney 2005). In pursuing growth through product innovation, companies should look at their customers as partners in creating and building value. Consumers today have near-instant access to all the information they need on virtually any product. Moreover, they use this information to influence product development as individuals, and more importantly, through user communities and review groups (Johnson 2006). Most companies ask their customers about their needs. Customers offer solutions in the form of products or services. Companies then deliver these tangibles, and customers may change their preference as the product or service is made available in the market.

Consumer perceptions play a key role in the lifecycle of a brand. The role varies according to the stage in the lifecycle, market situation, and competitive scenario. A company to invest on appealing communication strategies for creating awareness may need to influence the decision of consumers toward buying the brands they have not tested before. Systematically explored concepts in the field of customer value and market-driven approach toward new products would be beneficial for a company to derive long-term profit optimization strategy over the period. On a tactical level, managers need to consider the optimum spread of customers on a matrix of product attractiveness and market coverage. This needs careful attention and application of managerial judgment and experience to measure the customer value-driven performance of the retail stores, considering the innovative sales approaches for organic products, store layouts, product displays supported with comprehensive point-of-sales information, brand information, and other loyalty parameters of the consumers.

Critical Path Analysis

CPM is one of the frequently used techniques in project planning in optimizing the task-time convergence. A typical project has many tasks involving different people, which often makes a project manager keep track of things. It is far too easy for certain activities to fall behind and get lost in the sea of endless jobs. CPM helps managers to determine the time span in completing the project and performing critical tasks manage the project budget and time schedules. The Program Evaluation and Review Technique (PERT) and CPM techniques are used in scheduling of activities that construct a project and to determine the earliest or latest start and finish schedules for each activity. These techniques would also help the project team in determining the entire project completion time and the slack time for each activity. Though PERT and CPM are similar in their basic approach, they do differ in the way activity times are estimated. Each activity monitored under PERT is classified as optimistic, or pessimistic, which is most likely to determine the expected activities to be carried out in the project determining the completion time and its variance. Thus, PERT is considered to be a probabilistic technique, which allows the project team to find the probability of the entire project being completed by any given date, and follow a deterministic approach by using two-time estimate, the normal time, and the crash time, for each activity during the project. The application of CPM is explained in Figure 5.2 in reference to an example of the project on innovative combustion control devise for automobiles.

The example of combustion control devise for automobiles for products like "start-stop" devise of Bosch GmbH, Germany, illustrated in Figure 5.2, shows the tasks T1 to T15 distributed in project in order of operational sequence that have many subtasks indicated with the arrows corresponding to the tasks. It is important for the project managers to review the tasks and subtasks in the project and apply CPM to eliminate the low-priority and repetitive tasks to reduce the time required for project completion as well as lower the real cost against those estimated. In the preceding illustration, the subtasks like T1A, T1B, T1C need to be prioritized and decided about which tasks to be performed to move to the task and subtasks 2A and 2B and subsequently to T3A. The CPM analysis suggests which subtasks to skip and which ones to "bridge" like T3A to T5A and T10A to T14A. The "bridges," if approved, would allow the project team to skip T4, T4A, T11, T12, and T13, including their subtasks and reach the completion of the project ahead of 26 weeks and could reduce the corresponding costs in managing those tasks. It is important to note that at the beginning of the project, the time taken for each task is the estimated time. During the project, the estimated time might vary based on different factors. In such cases, it is important to revisit the CPM diagram and again do a critical path analysis. Experienced developers are usually accurate with their estimations, so time overrun is not something that will happen frequently. It is essential to estimate

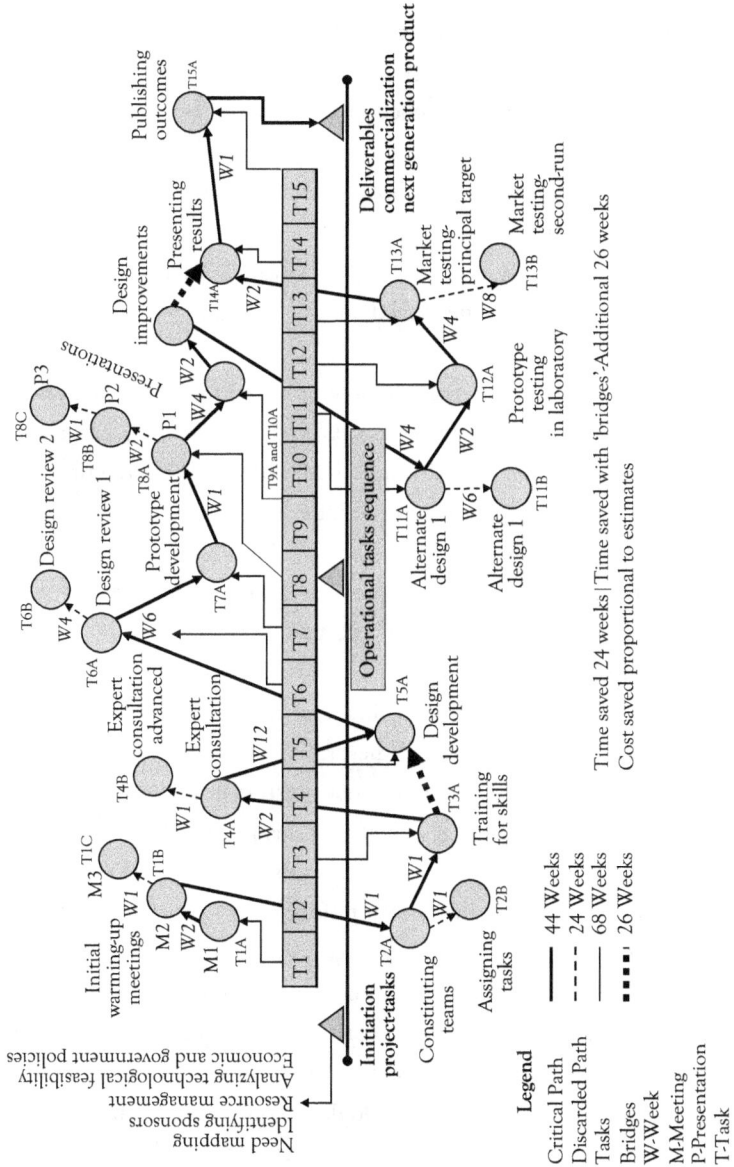

Figure 5.2 *Application of critical path method*

the time needed for each subtask when planning any project to calculate. This helps to establish the start date of any activity, which cannot start until the preceding activity has been completed. The calculations also determine the latest date for completion of an activity, so that the next activity can begin. Benefits of using a PERT chart or the CPM include:

- Improving planning and scheduling of activities
- Managing project cost and deliverables
- Simplifying the planning process by identification of repetitive planning patterns
- Managing expected project completion time, probability of completion before a specified date

CPM is a powerful but basically a simple technique for analyzing, planning, and scheduling large, complex projects. This tool provides a means of determining which jobs or activities in a project are critical in their effect on total project time, and guides to schedule all jobs in the project in the best possible order to complete it on schedule and within the minimum cost. The innovation projects should be analyzed through CPM, explaining the description of the task, date of completion, and periodical schedule of progress reporting. The tasks may also be started and stopped independent of each other, and must be performed in the order of priority for completion of the project successfully. The concept of CPM is quite simple and may be best illustrated in terms of a project graph, which is valuable in depicting visually and clearly the complex tasks in a project and their interrelations with the other tasks. In order to carry out CPM analysis, each task necessary for the completion of a project should be listed with unique identification using alphanumeric codes, with specific time requirement to complete the task, and its immediate prerequisites. For convenience in graphing, and as a check on certain kinds of data errors, the tasks may be arranged in the order of priority in reference to the technological requirements. There would be an error in technological ordering if a cycle error exists in the tasks data (like task a precedes b, b precedes c, and c precedes a). Further, each task is drawn on the graph as a circle, with its identifying symbol and time appearing within the circle. Sequence relationships are indicated by arrows connecting task with its immediate successors, with the arrows pointing to the latter. The critical path can be best understood as the bottleneck route to complete the project in lesser time and cost against that has been projected. Only by finding ways to shorten the time to perform tasks through the critical path, the overall project time can be reduced in innovation projects. CPM helps project managers eliminate the noncritical jobs to perform that are irrelevant from the viewpoint of total project time, cost, quality, and deliverables (Levy, Thompson, and Wiest 1963). Using CPM, project managers can avoid poor planning of projects by visualizing the important tasks of a project depicted in the CPM chart. The main aim is to produce a visual of the entire project broken down into smaller activities, which are vital to the completion of the entire project. The benefits of applying CPM to each set of the tasks include:

- Predicting the time each activity will take and offering a timescale to the client
- Seeing how each section is important to the drive the progress of the project
- Assigning the right team to carry out the tasks and the concerned department to monitor the critical and corresponding tasks

All innovation projects should identify the specific tasks and milestones. Milestones are the events that mark the beginning and the end of one or more tasks. The network diagram (CPM chart) contains the sequence of the successive and parallel activities. In the diagram, arrowed lines represent the activities and circles or "bubbles" represent milestones. Weeks are a commonly used unit of time for activity completion, but any consistent unit of time can be used. For each task, the CPM model usually includes three time estimates:

- Optimistic time—the shortest time in which the activity can be completed
- Most likely time—the completion time having the highest probability
- Pessimistic time—the longest time that an activity may take

Accordingly, the expected time for each task can be calculated using the following weighted average equation:

$$E_t = \frac{\left[O_t + 4\left(M_{lt}\right) + P_t\right]}{6}$$

In the preceding equation E_t denotes the expected time, O_t and M_{lt} indicate optimistic and most likely time, respectively, and P_t is expressed for pessimistic time. The statistical weight for each time variable is used from 1 to 4, and some of the weights serve as the denominator in the preceding equation. Analyzing the expected time helps to bias time estimates away from the unrealistically short timescales normally assumed. The critical path is determined by adding the times for the activities in each sequence and determining the longest path in the project. The critical path determines the total calendar time required for the project. The amount of time that a noncritical path activity can be delayed without delaying the project is referred to as slack time. In the CPM, projects managers should determine the following four times for each task:

- ES—earliest start time
- EF—earliest finish time
- LS—latest start time
- LF—fastest finish time

These time units are calculated using the expected time for the relevant activities. The earliest start and finish times of each activity are determined by working forward through the network and determining the earliest time at which an activity can start and finish, considering its predecessor activities. The latest start and finish times are the latest times that an activity can start and finish, without delaying the project. LS and LF are found by working backward through the network. The difference in the latest and earliest finish of each activity is that activity's slack. The critical path then is the path through the network in which none of the activities have slack.

CPM is considered as one of the major quantitative tools for business decision making. It is a simple technique for analyzing, planning, and development of complex products and for completing them at minimum cost (Jassawalla and Sahsittal 2000). Analysis by CPM may be applied to new product development or product innovation projects that have three common characteristics essential for CPM analysis—the product development information consists of some well-defined process determinants; the process may be started or stopped independently of each other, within a given sequence; and the product development process must be performed in technological sequence. A step-by-step analysis might demonstrate critical path scheduling and the process of constructing a graph. CPM is a schedule network analysis technique. CPM was developed by the DuPont Corporation in 1957. Critical path determines the shortest time to complete the project, and it is the longest duration path through a network of tasks. It may be viewed from the preceding figure that CPM is based on the creation of a sequence of dependent tasks (i.e., tasks that can only be performed after earlier tasks are complete). Performing critical path analysis on this sequence allows managers to work out possible parallel sequences (i.e., tasks that can be performed simultaneously). The critical path is the longest chain of dependent tasks required for product development. The benefits of CPM in product development process include:

- Production planning and control
- Time-cost trade-offs
- Cost-benefit analysis
- Contingency planning
- Reducing risk

It is important to analyze the feedback in each stage in the process of product development. The power of analytics in decision making is well-recognized in the process monitoring and evaluation stages, but few companies have what it takes to successfully implement a complex analytics program. Most firms will get greater value from learning through feedback in various stages of the product development process. Managers need to become adept at routinely using techniques employed by scientists and medical researchers. Specifically, they need to embrace the "test and learn" approach by way of taking one action with one group of customers, a different action (or no action at all) with a control group of customers, and then compare the results. The feedback from even a handful of experiments can yield immediate and dramatic improvements (Anderson and Simester 2011).

Companies must identify core competencies, which provide potential access to a wide variety of markets, make a contribution to the customer benefits of the product, and are difficult for competitors to imitate. In a later stage, firms must reorganize to learn from alliances and focus on internal development (Prahalad and Hamel 1990). Determining the set of competencies required by different positions is a monumental task, and it requires input from all levels of an organization. Managers need to look into the legitimate control of the costs, improve the operational dynamics, and quality of product. It has been argued that new frontier in value creation is emerging with fresh opportunities in a competitive marketplace. In this new frontier, the role of the consumer has changed from isolated to connected, from unaware to informed, from passive to active. As a result, companies can no longer act autonomously, designing products, developing production processes, crafting marketing messages, and controlling sales channels with little or no interference from consumers. Armed with new tools and dissatisfied with available choices, consumers want to interact with firms and thereby co-create value. The use of interaction as a basis for co-creation is at the crux of emerging reality. The co-creation experience of the consumer becomes the very basis of value through a DART model for managing co-creation of value processes. The DART model has four constituents—dialog, access, risk assessment, and transparency. Combining the building blocks of transparency, risk assessment, access, and dialog enables companies to better engage customers as collaborators. Transparency facilitates collaborative dialog with consumers (Prahalad and Ramasway 2004).

Stage-Gate Process

In formulating project decision strategies, it is necessary to involve all role players, such as project team, sponsors, deliverables, quality and packaging managers, distributors, logistics and inventory managers, retailers, franchisees, and so on, and fully acquaint with the marketplace environment. The low involvement project team leads to poor project decisions and implementation; however, intensive feedback and business analysis on innovation projects are helpful in shaping project deliverables. Project strategists tend to use powerful drivers while referring to implementation efforts. Project managers should know that the implementation of project policy is a critical ally in building a capable organization, and use of the appropriate drivers of implementation of the innovative business projects is the pivotal hinge in the growth of business of a firm.

Innovation projects can benefit from opening up the customer-centric pricing development process to reap long-run advantage in the marketplace. They can co-create consumer-oriented pricing by integrating the consumer value with the stage-gate process. This decision process in project management explores opportunities for employing both inbound and outbound review of the expected project deliverables in reference to upstream and downstream markets. The stage-gate decision model can exploit the advantages of openness, economic rationale, and sustainable effect of decisions for achieving the project goals. This model would allow explicit consideration of managerial know-how and technology through gate evaluations and also enable the project team to continuously assess their core capabilities in working through this decision model. The stage-gate process in determining project decision from the initiation stage to the stage of completion is exhibited in Figure 5.3.

A stage-gate model is a conceptual and operational roadmap for developing an effective pricing strategy. This model divides the effort into distinct stages separated by management decision gates. Cross-functional teams must successfully complete a prescribed set of related cross-functional tasks in each stage, prior to obtaining management

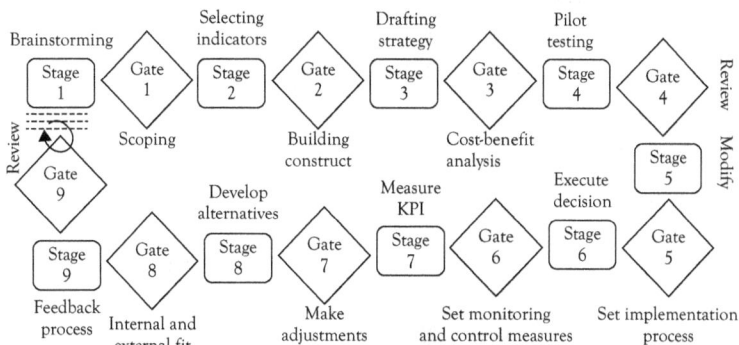

Figure 5.3 Stage-gate model for decision making

approval to proceed to the next stage of product development. The stage-gate processes have a great deal of appeal to price management, because, basically, they restrict investment in the next stage until management is comfortable with the outcome of the current stage. The gate can be effective in controlling product quality and development expense. Stages and gates in the project decisions are sequential phases and may run into some overlapping activities, especially when they cross the decision points. The stage-gate process leads toward completing tasks sequentially step by step. A newer alternative to the stage-gate process is CPM, which is essentially a management by exceptions technique, in which certain critical parameters of the project, such as cost, time, risk, product performance level, and deliverables are managed by reducing the cost, shortening the time, and delivering quality outputs. Firms need to conduct regular checks so that the project teams remain within bounds. The criteria used in the gate review involve aspects such as:

- Strategic decision fit in the project environment
- Project attractiveness in reference to cost, time, deliverables, risk, and profit
- Competitive advantage
- Anticipated response level of project team

The stage-gate process begins with understanding the market demand, consumer needs, and project resources for developing an appropriate project decision strategy. Tasks associated with the development of a good project task and time line are then divided into a sequence of logical steps called *stages*, each of which is preceded by a *gate* where the attractiveness of the project is assessed. During each stage, a cross-functional project team carries out tasks that result in the completion of defined deliverables including those related to technical (manufacturing, R&D, quality, regulatory) and business (sales, marketing, business development) functions. The advantages of using the stage-gate process are as follows:

- Improved project performance
- Shorter project time
- Quality project deliverables

- Earlier detection of conflicts during review in gates
- Less recycling and rework

Innovative business projects combined with strategic business initiatives involve significant market and customer attraction. Some innovation-led projects fail because the existing project management methods are unable to forecast their commercial success accurately. Firms managing innovation projects also need to develop systems thinking in managing projects and apply the stage-gate process method to capitalize on the "power of wisdom of project" by allowing the project teams define the business-linked project rules. Such project management practices motivate project teams, sponsors, and project owners (organizations) to enhance boundary of project deliverables, commercialization, and customer value.

Cognitive Factors in Entrepreneurial Performance

Effective management of a firm typically requires both planning and control, establishing performance measuring and rewarding systems to reinforce specific goals of the organization, and developing mindsets of project managers by creating a sense of shared responsibility in performing tasks. Although companies invest considerable time and money to administer polices through project managers, it is necessary to focus on the management strategies on how the structure of the sales force needs to be closely associated with the performance indicators of a firm's business. Firms must consider the relationship between the differing roles of project managers in reference to intrinsic and extrinsic tasks, degree of specialization, and how to develop a corporate image. These factors are critical in measuring the efficacy of management because they determine how quickly a firm can respond to market opportunities, competitive goals, and reflect on revenues, costs, and profitability of the firm (Tsai, MacMillan, and Low 1991).

The task of a project manager changes over the course of the strategy administration process. Different abilities are required at each stage of management, including analysis of strengths, weaknesses, opportunities, and threats, creating solutions, and taking the lead. Success of the project managers depends on the knowledge, attitude, and practice that they need to have the SMART tag comprising qualities of being strategic, measurable, aggressive, responsive, and time-driven (Rajagopal and Rajagopal 2008). Project managers often view their tasks as a set of stereotypical activities, but in practice, it is a diligent task that involves a variety of conflicts and high risk. Hence, the performance of project managers is demonstrated by effective administrative skills not only in developing new ambiance to carry tasks effectively, but also to resolve conflicts and ambiguities during the task-handling process and dynamics. Result-oriented performance and control are positively related attributes of project managers that lead to the success of the organization (Hultink and Atuahene-Gima 2000).

The project managers' goals arise out of necessities rather than desires; they excel at defusing conflicts between individuals or departments, placating all sides while ensuring that an organization's day-to-day business gets done. Project managers should also possess the traits of a good leader to drive enthusiasm among employees of the organization and drive them in competitive dynamics. Leaders, on the other hand, adopt personal, active attitudes toward goals. They look for the opportunities and rewards that are available around, inspiring subordinates and firing up the creative process with their own energy. Their relationships with employees and coworkers are intense, and their working environment is often chaotic (Abraham 2004).

Personality Traits

Businesses organizations need both project managers and leaders to survive and succeed in the global competition. Project managers routinely overvalue certain skills and traits when it's time to hire, promote, or administratively support an employee. However, some organizations have the right behavioral perspectives in place to portray complete and accurate pictures of coherence and competence in a cross-cultural workplace. The seasoned and senior project managers reveal their competence by using a mysterious blend of psychological abilities known as emotional intelligence. Such managers are self-aware and empathetic.

Encouragement

A good project manager gives credit when it is due to his fellow workers and does not hog the credit. This trait of a good manager is sustaining over many years. It is essential for a project manager to understand the strategic insights or accomplishments made in the context of organizational growth and its goodness of fit in leveraging performance. In this way, project managers should exhibit the qualities also of a good learner in an organization. Direct learning derives from the manager's own experience and vicariously from the experience of others. In this learning process, a project manager discovers how to benefit from the suggested practice by fellow workers or his team members to prevent problems, create improvement opportunities, and rethink the way it does business (Cook and Brown 1999). Project managers also learn indirectly through the insights of fellow workers and functionaries of supporting organizations such as suppliers, customers, consultants, and competitors to understand and draw useful inferences about a practice. In either way of learning, a good manager always tends to acknowledge his team members for their contributions to organizational growth.

It is observed that most project managers in private firms have high trust in employees. While project managers in collective enterprises develop the lowest trust in employees, the managerial values of power, distance, and collectivism also affect the trust and work culture in business organizations (Wang 2002). Project managers should nurture the organizational values in a triadic portrait of 3A factors that include the personality traits of appreciation, acknowledging, and alluring. Learning to adapt to the advice of co-workers is the way of doing things, which actually helps project managers in maintaining control of the process of carrying tasks. Once project managers have that skill, they need never feel apprehensive about working with or for anyone (Simpson 2002).

Supervision and Functional Efficiency

Project managers represent a large chunk and increasing percentage of the employees of multinational companies. In various industrial segments like financial services, health care, high-technology products manufacturers, pharmaceuticals, and media and entertainment, managers constitute 25 percent or more of the workforce engaged in general-line activities. As most organizations are vertically oriented, the retrofitted organizational structure prompts managers to achieve objectives by pressure tactics on employees, which makes the workplace ambiance more complex. Thus, during the supervisory operations project managers tend to intervene in the task-handling process of peers and outsourced workers, which often lead to inefficient outcome performance. Project managers often choose to work with ad hoc and matrix overlays formed between the vertical structures that affect the functional efficiency in carrying tasks in an organization as well as hamper the organizational work culture (Bryan and Joyce 2005). Project managers in vertical organizations run into interference and attempt to solve problems at the higher level.

Time Management

One of the typical work cultures that Japanese have may be described as 3T power-grid, which comprises a synergy of task (commitment), thrust (driving force), and time (punctuality). Task, thrust, and time relationship is an important strategic triad to be understood by project managers. The theories of time management have progressed beyond these ideas, as the global competition among firms has grown over time. The goal of time management is to allow coworkers and team members to spend most of their time on work that is truly important, but relatively nonurgent. Work and leisure should both be governed by this same philosophy, by balancing excellence in work with excellence in relaxation (Billington 1997). Project managers should strategically manage time, providing staff with greater control over their professional time. The time structure plays a key role in building a performance-driven organization. Due to failures in complying with task schedules, growth opportunities are sometimes not fully realized. Spin-out time management is a process by which multiple tasks are distributed within a given time frame and monitored independently that enhances the individual's innovative capabilities in carrying out the task. Such time management practice is commonly followed by project managers in many multinational companies (Pieter and van Gorp 2003).

Responsiveness

Project managerial responsiveness is inculcated through effective listening to coworkers and subordinates, understanding the problem, and developing action-oriented thinking in an organization. Listening begins at home, which implies that good managers pay due attention to the ideas of their employees. Employees give lots of verbal and nonverbal messages about whether their concerns have been heard, and project managers need to respect their feelings. Generally speaking, the more important a communication is, the more important is the originator of the communication and that determines when a project manager listens to his or her employee. An attentive listener develops trust among employees and such confidence builds strength. In an organization where managers are good listeners, the employees share the tasks and achievements. Common understanding may be used as a filter to analyze solutions to problems emerging in the team. The information flow should be streamlined for drawing suitable interpretations, inferences, and implications. However, managerial culture is an omnipresent evolution of organizational behaviors that continually helps in building trust among different subgroups of employees in an organization (Rajagopal 2006).

Judicious

Rapidly changing work culture and complexities of organizational problems demand a quick and judicious managerial decision to drive toward a win-win situation. Fast-cycle decision making is not just about making decisions more quickly. It is a rethinking of the decision-making model, where managerial intuition is combined with employees performing brainstorming discussions, carrying out task simulations, and sharing information among the peers. Experiences of project managers drawn from several companies and leading management studies suggest that the managers' ability to act quickly and wisely depends on his or her personality traits, problem-solving abilities, and managerial relations with the employees (Prewitt 1998). The tolerance limit for any ambiguity and uncertainty in the team work may be very narrow for a project manager while working in a team. This attitude of project managers also reflects their consciousness to the time frame associated with the task of the team.

It is required to fix the criteria for the team members to work in the team on the assigned tasks, set a judgmental framework, and detect fallacies (van Woerkom and van Engen 2009). It is may also be necessary to produce a new combination of roles, considering originality or creativity to protect individualism and reduce any assertiveness among the coworkers and staff members.

The value of managerial judgment is an analytical tool that provides a useful way of focusing on creative accomplishments in an organization, rather than their rational limitations because of manager-staff relations or organizational policies. In doing so, project managers should reassert the value of the word "policy" in an organization in reference to its connotations of instrumentality, functionality, and linear rationality (Brownlie 1998). Unsuccessful decisions that were mismatched to the decision task can be explored by project managers to uncover what went wrong and discover ways to improve the chance of success (Nutt 2002).

Proactive and Helpful

The human-value system is a synergy of societal values, family values, and individual values generated through the influence of culture. The personality traits of project managers are largely evolved through family and societal values that govern the family-value paradigm. As regards taking interest in the achievement of each member as well as of the group, the project managers should exhibit a positive attitude to motivate the staff (Cumming 1980). In a work environment, it would be challenging for a project manager to understand and adapt to individual behavior of different cultural groups and use a yardstick to soften the communication gap. Japanese believe in implicit communication with the rule-of-thumb that implied is better than spoken and that employees should appreciate interdependence to work in an organization effectively (Haru 1997).

Resource Management

In practice, project managers need to predict how alternative and relatively complex strategies or administrative processes affect dynamic results, and their likely impacts on employee morale and organizational growth. This is why managers typically obtain key employees' prior reactions to any new decision, policy or operational approach, and pretest the new idea on a limited scale. These procedures, however, may not provide accurate long-run predictions, and they can be applied to only one or two ideas at a time (Darmon 1997). The decision of project managers based on collective resources determines the task distribution and rewarding dimensions within a predetermined control process. Such strategies operate independently from managers' monitoring, directing, and evaluating activities, and needs to be assessed separately in the practice of management (Lawler 1990). Project managers should be resourceful in increasing the knowledge of their staff by arranging training in relevant areas directed to boost their capabilities and skills. Project managers need to focus on removing implied status barriers between sales and customer value—a strategic direction to help salespeople to build stronger values to overcome cultural diversities and optimize results. It is also important for the managers to train salespeople toward managing customer emotions, collective competence, and ethical complexities (Martin and Bush 2003).

Creativity

Principles of the relational-cultural theory indicate that the role of relational competency is important in fostering the growth of employees and organization. One of the principal goals is to identify and define specific relational competencies that support creative, innovative, inclusive, and relational practice (Duffey, Haberstroh, and Trepal 2009). One of the attributes of a good manager is to be creative in managing tasks and employee relationships. Managerial creativity aggregates the roles of the cognitive, motivational, and social processes of managing an organization to instill innovation among the coworkers and teams (Paulus and Dzindolet 2008). These attributes of mangers distinguish them from most of the existing work cultures across the countries in the world. This has reflected into the material culture (technology and economy) of Japan toward continues improvement (Kaizen). In fact, Kaizen is a form of creativity embedded in social culture, which has been adapted by Japanese organizations. Japan is a more centralized society that lays emphasis on Darwinian philosophy of evolution—survival of the fittest, which sets more rigid standards of work culture leading to Kaizen (Haru 1997). A good project manager should be able to create an aura among employees to express creative thinking. Aura is defined as a cover that is related to the feeling—experiences of beauty, exclusiveness, uniqueness, and authenticity that an idea, thought process, or imagination creates in an organization. Creativity is an intangible asset for a project manager and a guiding tool for an organization (Björkman 2002). Managing creativity has two serious challenges that managers face in increasing the creativity of their organizations. The objective of managing creativity is to cultivate a creative approach and curiosity in life and work, challenge and test our current mental models, and engage in active experimentation with new mindsets and approaches.

Project managers of emerging companies may have a long-standing and pertinent question of how to map the cognitive variables of employees and develop a coherent work culture. This issue is very pertinent to the organizations that have cross-cultural workplace environment. Behavioral skills and administrative competencies of a project manager are strongly associated with the performance and organizational growth. Higher dependency on the superiors in making decisions on administrative matters lowers the cognitive inertia of project managers in a growing firm and affects the internal fit of working environment in an organization. Hence, the project managers may be delegated higher autonomy in phased manner during the *growth* stage of the firm. However, effective implementation of autonomy requires a clear view of the objectives, dedication toward understanding cognitive dimensions of employees, and developing discipline at work. A successful project manager should lean toward conducting behavioral analysis of employees, acquire skills in managing manpower, develop commitment, and build network within workplace in reference to task, time, thrust, and target (Rajagopal, Banks, and Rajagopal 2011).

References

Abraham, Z. 2004. "Managers and Leaders: Are they Different." *Harvard Business Review* 82, no. 1, pp. 74–81.

Anderson, E.T., and D. Simester. 2011. "A Step-by-Step Guide to Smart Business Experiments." *Harvard Business Review* 89, no. 3, pp. 124–32.

Billington, J. 1997. "Fairly Timeless Insights on How to Manage Your Time." *Harvard Business Publishing Newsletter*, February, 1–2.

Björkman, I. 2002. "Aura: Aesthetic Business Creativity." *Consumption Markets & Culture* 5, no. 1, pp. 69–78.

Bryan, L.L., and C. Joyce. 2005. "21st Century Organizations." *McKinsey Quarterly Online* August.

Brownlie, D. 1998. "High Minds and Low Deeds: On Being Blind to Creativity in Strategic Marketing." *Journal of Strategic Marketing* 6, no. 2, pp. 117–30.

Browning, T., and R.V. Ramasesh. 2015. "Reducing Unwelcome Surprises in Project Management." *MIT Sloan Management Review* 56, no. 3, pp. 53–62.

Cook, S.D.N., and J.S. Brown. 1999. "Bridging Epistemologies: The Generative Dance Between Organizational Knowledge and Organizational Knowing." *Organization Science* 10, no. 4, pp. 381–400.

Cristiano, J.J., J.K. Liker, and C.C. White III. 2000. "Customer-Driven Product Development Through Quality Function Deployment in the U.S. and Japan." *Journal of Product Innovation Management* 17, no. 4, pp. 286–308.

Cummings, T. 1980. *Systems Theory for Organizational Development*, 19–25. Chi Chester, UK: Wiley.

Cummings, J., and C. Pletcher. 2011. "Why Project Networks Beat Project Teams?" *MIT Sloan Management Review* 52, no. 3, pp. 75–80.

Darmon, R.Y. 1997. "Predicting the Long-Run Profit Impact of a Contemplated Sales Force Compensation Plan." *Journal of the Operational Research Society* 48, no. 1, pp. 1215–25.

Duffey, T., S. Haberstroh, and H. Trepal. 2009. "A Grounded Theory of Relational Competencies and Creativity in Counseling: Beginning the Dialogue." *Journal of Creativity in Mental Health* 4, no. 2, pp. 89–112.

Hartmann, P., and V.I. Apaolaza. 2006. "Green Value Added." *Marketing Intelligence & Planning* 24, no. 7, pp. 673–80.

Haru, Y. 1997. *Different Games Different Rules*, 54–55. New York: Oxford University Press.

Hultink, E.J., and K. Atuahene-Gima. 2000. "The Effect of Sales Team Adoption on New Product Selling Performance." *Journal of Product Innovation Management* 17, no. 6, pp. 435–50.

Iyer, B., and T.H. Davenport. 2008. "Reverse Engineering Google's Innovation Machine." *Harvard Business Review* 86, no. 4, pp. 59–68.

Jassawalla, A.R., and C.H. Sashittal. 2000. "Strategy of Effective New Product Team Leaders." *California Management Review* 42, no. 2, pp. 34–41.

Johnson, L.K. November 2006. *Harnessing the Power of the Customer*, 1–2. Cambridge, MA: Harvard Business Publishing Newsletter, Harvard Business School Publishing.

Lafferty, B.A., and R.E. Goldsmith. 2004. "How Influential are Corporate Credibility and Endorser Attractiveness When Innovators React to

Advertisement for a New High Technology Product?" *Corporate Reputation Review* 7, no. 1, pp. 24–26.

Lamming, R.C., T.E. Johnsen, C.M. Harland, and J. Zheng. May 2000. "Managing in Supply Networks: Cascade and Intervention." *9th International Annual IPSERA Conference Proceedings.* University of Western Ontario, Canada, 24–27.

Laroche, M., J. Bergeron, and G. Barbaro-Forleo. 2001. "Targeting Consumers Who are Willing to Pay More for Environmentally Friendly Products." *Journal of Consumer Marketing* 18, no. 6, pp. 503–20.

Lawler, E.E. 1990. *Strategic Pay: Aligning Organizational Strategies and Pay Systems.* San Francisco, CA: Jossey-Bass.

Levy, F.K., G.L. Thompson, and J.D. Wiest. 1963. "ABCs of the Critical Path Method." *Harvard Business Review* 41, no. 5, pp. 98–108.

Martin, C.A., and A.J. Bush. 2003. "The Potential Influence of Organizational and Personal Variables on Customer-Oriented Selling." *Journal of Business and Industrial Marketing* 18, no. 2, pp. 114–32.

Mohammed, K.F., and A.A. Aibinu. March 29, 2013. "Managing Project Scope Definition to Improve Stakeholders' Participation and Enhance Project Outcome." *Procedia—Social and Behavioral Sciences* 74, pp. 154–64.

Nutt, P.C. 2002. "Making Strategic Choices." *Journal of Management Studies* 3, no. 1, pp. 67–96.

Paladino, A. 2005. "Understanding the Green Consumerism: An Empirical Analysis." *Journal of Customer Behaviour* 4, no. 1, pp. 69–102.

Paulus, P.B., and M. Dzindolet. 2008. "Social Influence, Creativity and Innovation." *Social Influence* 3, no. 4, pp. 228–47.

Pieter, K.J., and D.M. van Gorp. 2003. "Spin-Out Management: Theory and Practice." *Business Horizons* 46, no. 2, pp. 15–24.

Prahalad, C.K., and G. Hamel. 1990. "Core Competence of the Corporation." *Harvard Business Review* 90, no. 3, pp. 79–91.

Prahalad, C.K., and V. Ramasway. 2004. *The Future of Competition: Co-Creating Unique Value with Customers.* Boston, MA: Harvard Business School Press.

Prewitt, E. August 1998. *Fast Cycle Decision Making* 1–2. Cambridge, MA: Harvard Business Publishing Newsletter.

Rajagopal. 2006. "Innovation and Business Growth through Corporate Venturing in Latin America: Analysis of Strategic Fit." *Management Decision* 44, no. 5, pp. 703–18.

Rajagopal. 2012. *Systems Thinking and Process Dynamics for Marketing Systems: Technologies and Applications for Decision Management.* Hershey, PA: IGI Global.

Rajagopal, and A. Rajagopal. 2008. "Team Performance and Control Process in Sales Organizations." *Team Performance Management* 14, no. 1, pp. 70–85.

Rajagopal, J. Banks, and A. Rajagopal. 2011. "Analyzing Cognitive Determinants in Managerial Decision Making." *International Journal of Business Excellence* 4, no. 1, pp. 44–60.

Sawhney, M., R.C. Wolcott, and I. Arroniz. 2006. "Different Ways for Companies to Innovate." *Sloan Management Review* 47, no. 3, pp. 74–81.

Simpson, L. August 2002. *Why Managing Up Matters.* Cambridge, MA: Harvard Management Update Newsletter.

Tsai, W.M., I.C. MacMillan, and M.B. Low. 1991. "Effects of Strategy and Environment on Corporate Venture Success in Industrial Markets." *Journal of Business Venturing* 6, no. 1, pp. 9–28.

van Woerkom, M., and M.L. van Engen. 2009. "Learning from Conflicts? The Relations Between Task and Relationship Conflicts, Team Learning and Team Performance." *European Journal of Work and Organizational Psychology* 18, no. 4, pp. 381–404.

Wang, Y. 2002. "Which Managers Trust Employees? Ownership Variation in China's Transitional Economy." *Asia Pacific Business Review* 9, no. 2, pp. 138–57.

Index

Accountability, 132
Adaptation of innovation, 57–67
Applied innovation, 54
Autonomous teams, 116

BCA. *See* Benefit-cost analysis
Benefit-cost analysis (BCA), 70
BEP. *See* Break-even point
Break-even point (BEP), 59
Business environment
    analyzing, 37–42
    globalization and, 1–6
Business innovation projects, 41
Business-system framework, 31

Chaos in market, 103–104
Commercialization, 32
Commitment as concept, 62
Communication, 143
Competitive differentiation, 6–12
Competitive intelligence
    in business firm, 11–13
    definition, 10
    perspectives, 11
Competitiveness, 140–145
Competitive strategy, 13
Constitution of project teams,
    105–108
Consumer-centric innovation, 15
Consumer-led innovations, 15, 33
Consumer perceptions, 167
Consumer Price Index (CPI), 68
Consumer purchasing motivations,
    162–163
Containerization, 142
Cost management, 93–95
Cost, time, and risk (CTR) factors,
    132
CPI. *See* Consumer Price Index
CPM. *See* Critical path method
CPV. *See* Customer preference and
    value
Creativity, 183–184

Critical path method (CPM)
    application of, 168–169
    benefits of applying, 171
    benefits of using PERT chart, 170
    overview of, 167–168
    product development process,
        173–174
    task determination, 172
    time estimates, 171
Critical success factors, 23–31
Customer-centric management, 60
Customer-centric strategies, 61
Customer preference and value
        (CPV), 158
Customer satisfaction, 63

Diffusion of innovation, 58–59
Discounted cash flow (DCF) model,
    94

Economic advancement, 68
Ecosystem of innovation, 32–33
Effectuation process, 81–82
11 Ps, marketing-mix strategies,
    160–161
Encouragement, 179
Entrepreneurial attributes, 73–75,
    81–91
Entrepreneurial mindset, 86–87, 89
Entrepreneurial performance
    creativity, 183–184
    encouragement, 179
    judicious managerial decision,
        181–182
    overview of, 177–178
    personality traits, 178
    proactive and helpful, 182
    resource management, 182–183
    responsiveness, 181
    supervision and functional
        efficiency, 179–180
    time management, 180
Entrepreneurship, 75–81

Existing demand, 69
Experience innovation, 46, 56
External project environment, 121–125

Family-based innovation, 88
Forming, 107
Functional efficiency, 179–180
Functionality-related competency, 30
Functional teams, 116

Globalization, 1–6, 100–103
Goal Oriented Project Planning (GOPP), 50
GOPP. *See* Goal Oriented Project Planning
Go-to-market (GTM) strategy, 63

Hub-and-spoke paradigm, 95
Human-value system, 182
Hybrid project teams, 134–135

IFG. *See* Innovation facilities group
Incipient demand, 69
Incremental innovation, 29
Industry-focused innovations, 15
Initiative for Policy Dialogue (IPD), 158
Innovation assimilation group, 122, 124
Innovation-driven companies, 3, 13
Innovation ecosystem, 32–33
Innovation entrepreneurship, 75–81
Innovation facilities group (IFG), 122
Innovation-imitation-equilibrium cycle, 30
Innovation-led product, 28–29
Innovation lifecycle, 160–167
Innovation performance
  ambience, 56
  competence, 56
  inputs, 55
  leadership, 55
  outputs, 55
  pipeline concepts, 55
  project balance, 56
Innovation project path, 86–87

Innovation strategy, 46
Innovative business projects
  attributes of, 47
  best practices, 51
  characteristics of, 47
  conventional phases, 52–53
  defining projects, 48–57
  exploring, 42–48
  geodemographic segments, 48
  managing projects, 48–57
  mission and goals, 76
  trends and organizational approaches, 18–23
  well-defined and comprehensive, 77
  work breakdown structure, 54
Integrity-related competency, 30
Internal project environment, 115–121
Internet of Things (IoT), 14
IoT. *See* Internet of Things
IPD. *See* Initiative for Policy Dialogue
IT-based innovations, 32

Judicious managerial decision, 181–182

Kaizen, 22–23, 183–184
Knowledge-based perspectives, 119
Knowledge management, 120

Latent demand, 69
Lean thinking, 104–105
Learning environment, 118
Localization process, 102

Macroeconomic factors, 41, 67–71
Market-access competency, 30
Market development, 97–104
Market entrepreneurship, 86
Marketing competitiveness, 144
Marketing-mix strategies, 41, 160–161
Microeconomic factors, 41–42, 67–71
Most likely time, 171
Multitask matrix, 131

New product development process,
165–166
NGO. *See* Nongovernment
organizations
Nongovernment organizations
(NGO), 20
Norming, 107

Open innovation, 22, 49
Open-market competition, 9
Optimistic time, 171
Organizational culture, 50
Organizational environment, 123
Organizational learning, 118
Outsourcing innovation process,
122–123

PCA. *See* Profit center approach
Performing, 107
Personality traits, 178
PERT. *See* Program Evaluation and
Review Technique
Pessimistic time, 171
Positioning, 65
Power equilibrium, 133
PPI. *See* Producer Price Index
PPM. *See* Project planning matrix
Producer Price Index (PPI), 68
Product innovation, 26–28
Product strategies, 65
Profit center approach (PCA), 63
Program Evaluation and Review
Technique (PERT), 167–168
Project administration, 113–115
Project charter, 50
attributes, 155–156
principal uses of, 159
resources, 159–160
Project environment
administration, 113–115
external, 121–125
internal, 115–121
Project lifecycle, 137–140
Project managerial responsiveness,
181
Project matrix, 130–137
Project network, 155

Project planning matrix (PPM), 132
Project scope
attributes and effects, 153–154
definition, 148–149
external dimensions, 151
outcomes, 150
tools and techniques, 150–151
Project scope verification, 151
Project team control, 106
Project team members attributes, 133
Project teams, 105–108
Public-private innovation, 21

QFD. *See* Quality Function
Deployment
Quality Function Deployment
(QFD), 164–165

Relational-cultural theory, 183
Resource management, 91–93,
182–183
Responsiveness, 181
Reverse innovation, 31
Risk aversion, 163
Robust network foundation, 127

Scope creep, 153–154
Scope management, 139
Shadow strategy task force, 29
Single-location projects, 56
Sociocommercial ecology, 125
SOW. *See* Statement of work
Spin-out time management, 180
Stage-gate process, 174–177
Start-up enterprises (SUEs), 33, 44,
74, 77, 90, 95, 121, 138
Statement of work (SOW), 49
Storming, 107
SUEs. *See* Start-up enterprises
Supervision, 179–180
Sustainable innovation, 75
Systematically explored concepts, 167

Team control, 106
Team management, 106
Team size, 133
Technological upgrading, 142

Technology marketing, 135
Technology-marketing efficiency, 63
TIC effect, 61
Time management, 180
Top-down decision approach, 116
Total Quality Control (TQC), 165
TQC. *See* Total Quality Control
Transfer of technology, 125–129
Transforming buying behavior, 126
Tryvertising, 128

Warming, 107
WBS. *See* Work breakdown
    structure
Work breakdown structure (WBS),
    54, 95–97
Work ethics, 117–118
Working relationship,
    115–116

Zero defects, 30

OTHER TITLES IN OUR PORTFOLIO AND PROJECT MANAGEMENT COLLECTION

Timothy J. Kloppenborg, Editor

- *Making Projects Sing: A Musical Perspective of Project Management* by Raji Sivaraman and Chris Wilson
- *Agile Project Management for Business Transformation Success* by Milan Frankl and Paul Paquette
- *Leveraging Business Analysis for Project Success* by Vicki James
- *Project Portfolio Management: A Model for Improved Decision Making* by Clive N. Enoch
- *Project Management Essentials* by Kathryn Wells and Timothy J. Kloppenborg
- *The Agile Edge: Managing Projects Effectively Using Agile Scrum* by Brian Vanderjack
- *Project Teams: A Structured Development Approach* by Vittal S. Anantatmula
- *Attributes of Project-Friendly Enterprises* by Vittal S. Anantatmula and Parviz F. Rad
- *Stakeholder-led Project Management: Changing the Way We Manage Projects* by Louise M. Worsley

Announcing the Business Expert Press Digital Library

Concise e-books business students need for classroom and research

This book can also be purchased in an e-book collection by your library as

- a one-time purchase,
- that is owned forever,
- allows for simultaneous readers,
- has no restrictions on printing, and
- can be downloaded as PDFs from within the library community.

Our digital library collections are a great solution to beat the rising cost of textbooks. E-books can be loaded into their course management systems or onto students' e-book readers.
The **Business Expert Press** digital libraries are very affordable, with no obligation to buy in future years. For more information, please visit **www.businessexpertpress.com/librarians**. To set up a trial in the United States, please email **sales@businessexpertpress.com**.

www.ingramcontent.com/pod-product-compliance
Lightning Source LLC
Chambersburg PA
CBHW072307210326
41519CB00057B/3048